THE HAWAIIAN SURVIVAL HANDBOOK

THE
HAWAIIAN
SURVIVAL
HANDBOOK

BY BROTHER NOLAND

ILLUSTRATIONS BY
ANDREW J. CATANZARITI

WATERMARK
PUBLISHING

ISBN: 978-1-935690-45-0

Library of Congress Control Number: 2014941674

The information in this book is meant to inform and educate and is not intended to be used as medical or other professional advice. No treatment presented herein is meant to diagnose, prevent or cure any disease, injury or other malady. Consuming food or water collected in the wild may carry risks. Always take proper safety precautions. Outdoor activities such as hunting, fishing or harvesting natural resources are subject to state, county and/or U.S. government regulations, and even frequently used trails and wilderness areas may require access to private property or unsafe terrain. Neither the publisher nor the author assumes any liability for injury or illness, or for any legal action, that may result from use of the contents of this book.

Watermark Publishing
1000 Bishop Street, Suite 806
Honolulu, HI 96813
Telephone: Toll-free 1-866-900-BOOK
Website: www.bookshawaii.net
e-mail: sales@bookshawaii.net

Printed in Korea

10 9 8 7

DEDICATION

For my legacy
You are why I survive...
We are why we survive...

For my children
and grandchildren:

Pomaikaimahina

Keahiamauloaokanoholani

Keiliahipua

Kamakalaukauikaiuokalani

Kaleoakalaniwahamana

Kealailiahi

CONTENTS

PREFACE

C hances are you won't ever have to escape a charging wild boar, or make a fire without matches, or fight off a tiger shark. These days, for those lucky enough to call Hawai'i home—or to vacation in the Islands—the danger zone doesn't go much beyond losing Wi-Fi or running out of mai tai mix. But even if you never find yourself fighting an undertow or tracking a deer, it can be a real adventure just reading about such survival skills from the comfort of your beach chair. What are the odds you'll ever have to find water underground or field dress a wild turkey? Not high, to be sure. But of course, you never know!

So who is your native guide to all this local knowledge? He's the legendary Hawaiian musician known simply as Brother Noland, who also happens to be an expert outdoorsman. Brother Noland has spent a lifetime surrounded by Hawai'i's forests, shorelines and oceans, and has also traveled far and wide to learn from expert native trackers in other cultures. He takes great joy in sharing his knowledge with others and considers it an important responsibility to educate the next generation.

In 1996, Brother Noland founded Hawaiian Inside Tracking (HIT), a high-impact, life-enhancing program that guides children from all walks of life into the great outdoors—removing them from their routine environment and usual comfort zones—to teach them the lessons of nature. The HIT program is offered by Brother Noland's Hō'ea Initiative (www.hoeainitiative.net), which gives adults and kids a chance to learn traditional Hawaiian tracking and survival skills. These nature camps perpetuate local knowledge, handing down traditional tools and concepts that are especially useful on islands: permission, conservation, preservation, sharing and sustaining life—not just for individuals, but for the greater community.

The Hawaiian Survival Handbook is a one-of-a-kind collection of beginner-level skills and techniques taught in the HIT program by Brother Noland and his staff: Jenny Yagodich, Palakiko Yagodich, Mele Coelho and Pomai Weigert, one of Brother Noland's daughters. Together, these skills constitute a unique guide to survival in the islands of Hawaiʻi.

You'll probably never need them. But then again, you never know!

INTRODUCTION

What does it mean to be a survivor? Survival can mean many different things. I remind the children and adults I teach that there are all kinds of smarts—brain smart, street smart, bush smart, suffering smart, athletic smart, business smart—and the *aloha* spirit is key to using all of them together for survival. A good sense of aloha keeps you open to learning as many "smarts" as you can. Your ego won't get in the way because learning and listening is what aloha is all about. That's how I learned to survive.

Survival began for me at an early age—just seven years old. It was 1964 and I was in the second grade, getting into fights at school, defending myself from bullying because my parents' idea of a haircut was to shave my head bald. Later that year, during the Christmas season—Christmas Eve, in fact—Dad decided to go AWOL and my parents called it quits. Of course, the impact of divorce can be devastating and detrimental to the psyche of any young child. Yet for me, something magical occurred. I would later understand it as a journey—call it an adventure or a walkabout. I would come to realize how blessed I was to have so many wonderful and caring teachers, mentors, family members and friends foster me during this difficult time.

Throughout my life I have practiced the art of listening. And I have also been as stubborn and ornery as a mule. But all of this has a way of coming together. To listen and learn, to be resilient and persevere, to use past experience and common sense to piece together what is happening now—all of these are innate qualities that can shape the character of a survivor.

In my childhood and as an adult, I have encountered many different extreme and over-the-top life situations—in the inner city, in the natural world, in my travels abroad, in my day-to-day life—many of them precarious. You could say I'm a guy who has pushed the envelope a time or two and has miraculously survived. I don't claim to know everything, but I do know a lot about growing up in Hawai'i and doing things island-style. And now I can share some of these lessons with you.

Learning the lessons of aloha will ultimately increase your awareness skills. Aloha is how you live your life, how you treat people, what you are true to and what you stand for. Be helpful and grateful. Live to inspire. Strive to live aloha every day, so that you can handle any survival situation.

The lessons of aloha are lessons that can make you happy, healthy and strong, inside and out; that can help you adjust, fit, match and blend, no matter what comes your way. Such skills can only be developed and passed along by great teachers. I have been very fortunate to have had so many strong, knowledgeable people guide me down the path less traveled, and yet worth taking. For more than fifty years, I have gathered, logged and practiced these teachings, and sharing them with others helps me remember and perpetuate them. *The Hawaiian Survival Handbook* is a way to document this knowledge, to pass it along in a different format, so that others can use it as a starting point for their own personal growth.

Consider this an introduction to the survival skills and techniques, to the lifestyle and culture, of Hawai'i: basic outdoor skills, tips on ocean awareness, important ways to communicate with, navigate and blend into the natural world. My hope is that it will help you grow to be more open, flexible, responsible and respectful, wherever you go on walkabout in Hawai'i, or in the greater world.

With greatest aloha,
BROTHER NOLAND

"WE ARE TAUGHT BY OUR KŪPUNA THAT FROM THE MOMENT WE ENTER THE WATER, WE ACKNOWLEDGE ALL OF THE OCEAN'S INHABITANTS. WE ARE VISITORS IN THEIR HOME."

OCEAN SKILLS

HOW TO AVOID A SHARK ATTACK

Hawaiians consider the shark, the greatest and most feared predator of the ocean, to be sacred. The shark is family. The shark is a guardian. The shark has its territory. We honor the shark's ocean domain and conduct ourselves accordingly whenever we enter the water. We are taught by our *kūpuna* (elders) that from the moment we enter the water, we acknowledge all of the ocean's inhabitants. We are visitors in their home. Whenever one enters the domain of *manō* (the shark), here are a few important things to remember:

◈ It is always a good idea to go with a partner who is familiar with the area and the surroundings, whenever you enter the water to dive, snorkel, swim or surf.

◈ Sharks are hungriest in the early morning and late evening. Find a time in-between for active ocean recreation.

◈ Tide is always a factor: High tide means big fish and large predators are incoming, and low or receding tide is when they head back out to sea. Be careful not to get caught in the crossfire of this "changing of the guard." Always check the tide calendar and observe what the tide is doing.

◈ Shark attacks mostly occur just offshore. Sharks come cruising in because they're hungry and looking for food. They are attracted to bright shiny colors, movement, or familiar shapes of prey, so rapid, excited splashing and kicking is not advised! From below, a shark sees your boogie board or surfboard as a *honu* (green sea turtle), and turtles are a favored shark meal.

- ◈ When diving, be aware that sharks have excellent vision, day or night, and can see well in low-lit areas.

- ◈ Scientists and *kūpuna lawaiʻa* (veteran fisherman) know that sharks have an incredible sense of smell. They can smell blood a mile away. Pay attention to your fish dragline or stringer. It will attract a hungry shark. If it does, better to just share than provoke an attack.

- ◈ Do not swim if you are bleeding, including women in their menstrual moon cycle. In ancient times, women were *kapu* (forbidden) to enter the water during this time.

- ◈ Avoid ocean areas where commercial fishing boats throw *palu* (scraps) overboard. They can attract sharks like chum.

◈ Avoid entering the water if you see flocks of birds low over the water. This indicates the presence of schools of fish—a shark buffet.

◈ Sharks love murky, muddy water, such as after a heavy rain or flood. Avoid brown ocean water and wait for the ocean and shoreline to clear up before going into the water.

◈ Be aware: All sharks, if provoked, have the potential to attack, and all large sharks are dangerous.

HOW TO SURVIVE A SHARK ATTACK

I f none of the avoidance tips work and you still find yourself as prey for the predator, take the offensive.

◈ Use your fist or anything else you have in your hand—camera, mask or snorkel—to hit the shark in the eyes or the gills, the areas most sensitive to pain. Despite conventional wisdom, either of these areas is a better bet than striking the nose.

◈ A shark will persist only if it feels it has an advantage. Fighting back sends a message to the shark that you aren't just another defenseless marine organism.

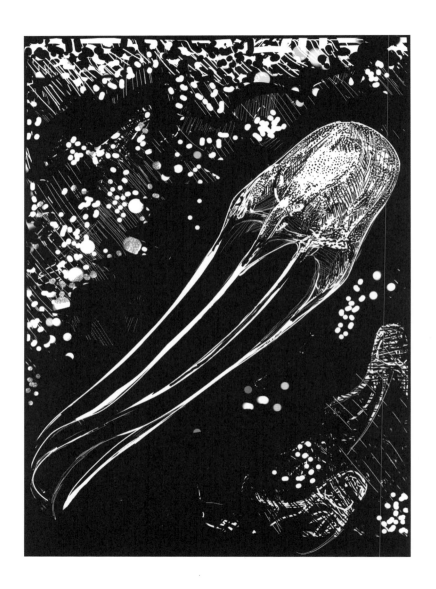

HOW TO DEAL WITH BOX JELLYFISH

The box jellyfish is an ocean creature whose presence in our shoreline waters is well-known among ocean-goers from surfers and swimmers to campers and fishermen. They primarily drift through the waters around the island of O'ahu. The main thing you have to remember is they will start to appear in abundance on the south and east shore waters eight to ten days after the full moon. However, they are always in our waters, and from time to time they can be on the west shore wrap, too, because of the wind direction and the push of the waves and currents. I have rarely heard of them appearing on the north side. No matter where you cruise in these islands, it's important to recognize and identify these critters. If you are busy foraging or just admiring the shoreline, it's easy to get distracted and not realize that you are entering box territory.

◈ Pay attention and make sure you can identify what a box jellyfish looks like. It blends in well in the shore break and bouncy white water.

◈ The body of a box looks like a small plastic bag floating in the water.

◈ Box jellyfish are usually blown in by the wind and currents, eventually drifting into our coastal waters. A lot of them end up on the beach as their final destination so watch where you step.

◈ During a jellyfish influx, they will hang around the area for about two to three days. It is a good idea to avoid the beach during this period. Go hiking instead.

◈ If you are completely submerged in water, remember that the majority of the jellyfish's body and them long stingers are also under the water. The stingers can be very lengthy and seem to float effortlessly like the hair of a horse's mane. If you see a box, assume the distance between you and the jellyfish contains its floating stingers and "get da hell outta Dodge."

◈ Don't sleep overnight right on the beach area where the tide and water level changes. You can end up sleeping in water with a few boxes as bed partners.

◈ If stung, you will have to scrape away or remove the stinger from your body. Don't attempt this with your bare hands. Look for a stick, rock or another kind of tool to remove it. This is to avoid getting stung again.

◈ To relieve the pain of a sting in a survival situation, use your pee. In a non-survival situation, look for your local lifeguard to assist, or head down to the closest convenience store or grocery outlet to get some vinegar. Put something cool on it afterwards for comfort. A soda bottle, *ti* leaf or any cold compress works great.

◈ A day or two after the pain goes away, the area will probably get itchy. You can use *laukahi* (plantain leaf; see page 136) to ease the itchiness, or an over-the-counter medicine.

HOW TO SURVIVE A RIPTIDE OR UNDERTOW

When we were kids, our grandparents (*tūtū wahine* and *tūtū kāne*) would sit us on the shoreline and teach us how to watch (*nānā*) and listen (*hoʻolohe*) to the ocean. We studied its patterns and movements, its currents and weather conditions. We also learned about the wind (*ka makani*) and the seabirds (*manu kai*). We even watched the debris return to shore to see where the gap exit, or *puka*, in the waves was in order to know how to float or swim safely back to shore.

Kai huki (undertow or rip current) is a dangerous shoreline condition, even for the strongest swimmer. **Undertow** is usually the backwash of a receding wave bouncing back from the next incoming wave underwater on the ocean bed. **Rip current** is almost the same thing—the receding water of a wave or the changing of tides channeled into a confined area, such as in between coral reefs, sandbars, rock formations and jetties. **Riptide** is the rising and falling of the tide in a constricted space where water will flow rapidly, like through a funnel or pipe.

All of these wave conditions are dangerous—not because you're pulled under the shoreline waters but because you can be pulled away from shore and sometimes out to sea. People drown because they are exhausted, panicked and unable to stay afloat. Don't swim alone, especially if you don't know the area well.

If you can't enter unfamiliar waters with someone with local knowledge, then sit on the shore and study the wave and current patterns for evidence of an undertow, rip current or riptide:

◈ Choppy, swirling white water in the channels, an obvious indication of dangerous conditions

◈ Ocean water that changes color dramatically

◈ Wave patterns moving differently within the regular incoming waves

If you do get caught in a riptide, rip current or undertow, here are some survival tips:

◈ Stay calm, think clearly and don't waste energy fighting or resisting the current.

◈ Swim out of the current parallel to the shoreline, feeling for that gap or opening in the water where you can turn to swim toward the shore.

◈ If you can't swim against the current, float and tread water calmly until you can feel the rip subside and then head for shore; use a backstroke if necessary.

◈ If all else fails and you are at an active beach with people on shore, raise and wave your arms and yell for help at the top of your lungs. (You'd be surprised at how quickly Hawai'i's ocean rescue personnel can reach distressed swimmers on their surfboards and jet skis.)

"PEOPLE DROWN BECAUSE THEY ARE EXHAUSTED, PANICKED AND UNABLE TO STAY AFLOAT. DON'T SWIM ALONE, ESPECIALLY IF YOU DON'T KNOW THE AREA WELL."

HOW TO MAKE A FLOTATION DEVICE

When you're surrounded by water, as we are in Hawai'i, this can be an important survival skill. This knowledge may be useful and even lifesaving in a catastrophic situation. Get creative with your own gear or use whatever Mother Nature might have on hand.

◈ Look for vegetation that will float. Fill a shirt or a pair of pants or, better yet, a sturdy plastic bag with vegetation, branches, grass or coconuts. (I always carry plastic bags on an outdoor trek; they always come in handy.) Tie the top tightly and use it as a raft. If you have rope, you can wrap it completely around the bag in a circle or half-circle to make a flotation device similar to a lifesaver or water wings.

◈ Find or cut two dry logs that are similar in size. Place them about two feet apart and lash them together. There should be enough rope between the logs to allow you to sit between them. Your legs go over one log and your arms over the other, with your butt in the water in between.

◈ Fill your poncho with vegetation and leaves, then fold it over and roll it like a sausage, tying it well to make it waterproof. You can carry this across your shoulders or around your waist.

◈ It's a sad commentary, but the litter people leave in the wild—especially plastic jugs, bottles and containers—can be useful in an emergency situation. Find containers with caps and no leaks. Large jugs can make a floating device. A *"lei"* of plastic water bottles strung together can make a serviceable flotation belt.

HOW TO FORAGE HAWAI'I'S SHORELINE

A lot of Hawaiians and locals refer to the ocean as their "icebox." Most shorelines in Hawai'i are abundant and rich with resources that can be foraged. It is extremely important to not over-harvest these resources so that they can replenish and not be depleted. Some shorelines, especially on O'ahu, have been brutally impacted by this kind of greedy behavior of cleaning out the icebox: wasting resources, polluting, destroying reefs, crowding a pristine environment, the list goes on... Shorelines are precious and many of those who use and depend on them are protective of their areas. Practice good protocol so as to avoid confrontations and realize that this is survival, too.

I'a is the general Hawaiian word for all resources found in the ocean and shoreline. Here are some of the edible creatures you can harvest and forage if you are in a survival situation or just want a learning experience. It's a good idea to go with someone who knows what to look for and teach you how to identify them.

SHELLFISH
There are numerous shellfish on a slow walk down a Hawai'i shoreline, I will share a few of the favorites.

⬥ *Pipipi*—small mollusks, tiny little shells found clinging to the rocks. You will have to harvest a lot for a fulfilling meal but they are easier to harvest off a rock than the *'opihi*. When we were kids growing up near the beach, one of our favorite things to do was to go with Tūtū Kāne and pick pipipi off the rocks. I used to just put 'um in my pants pocket 'til full. You remove the meat by using a needle. You can eat it raw, or you can boil them or make a soup. If you have access to fresh water, you can use that. If not, some ocean water would work, but would be real salty.

◈ 'Opihi—These favored limpets are so good they get their own section. See page 28.

◈ *Leho* or *Poleholeho*—The big or small cowry shell is an edible morsel as well. I grew up in Hawai'i learning to prize the leho as a beautiful ornament or piece of jewelry, but if you are in a survival situation, you can certainly harvest the creature. The living leho can usually be found on the ocean floor or under and between rocks hiding from its arch enemy, the *he'e* (octopus). To harvest the meat, you must crack the shell and carefully remove the animal. It is very slimy, so you will need to clean it by pouring salt on top and removing the guck. If you can find ti leaves, you can wrap and broil on hot coals, or you can boil the meat. This one, not so good to eat raw—I'm not even sure if you can, because I was never taught that.

SEAWEED

The general Hawaiian word for all seaweed is *limu*. They are broken down by different species, for example, *limu 'ele 'ele*, *limu kala*, etc. Hawaiian seaweeds are edible and rich in nutritional value, vitamins A, C, B12 and other mineral elements. It's important to be able to identify and distinguish the species before you just go around eating them, though. And make sure you wash and clean them. In our *'ohana* (family) limu is usually the fourth component to our meal along with *poi*, fish and meat. My favorite is beef stew with limu 'ele 'ele. All types of limu should be washed and cleaned, then pounded to break and cut in pieces. Eat in pinches.

◇ *Limu Kohu (Asparagopsis taxiformis)*—soft and small with furry topped branches; tan, pink or dark red

◇ *Limu Wawae'iole (Codium edule)*—dark green with a felt-like surface

◇ Limu 'Ele 'Ele *(Enteromorpha prolifera)*—looks like fine, green hairs; grows in tufts

◇ *Limu Huluhuluwaena (Grateloupia filicina)*—looks a little like ferns, with fine branches

◇ *Limu Lipoa (Dictyopteris plagiogramma)*—has wavy yellow-gold leaves and a dark center

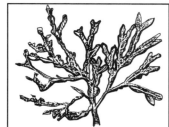

◇ *Limu Palahalaha (Ulva fasciata)*—looks like light green ribbons

CRABS

The general Hawaiian word for all crab is *papaʻi*. Of course, we already know how tasty these creatures can be. The trick is how to catch them. These three crabs can be eaten raw or cooked.

◈ *ʻAʻama*—ʻAʻama crab is the black crab found roaming in between the shoreline rocks or wharfs. Anywhere there are exposed rocks and reef you will usually find a clan of ʻaʻama. You can try and catch these critters in the day and have fun doing that, but when we were kids we would always harvest ʻaʻama crab at night, right off the rocks. They are usually out in big numbers during the night. This was always a fun adventure, but pay attention because rocky shorelines are slippery. Take a flashlight or make a torch and go torch fishing.

◈ *ʻAlamihi*—This is the crab that hangs in the *muliwai* (river mouth) or the mudflats. The usual way to catch these is with a *pokini* (a floating bucket) and a scoop net. But if you're in a survival situation, this is what you do: Walk the edges of the river and near mangroves observing movement and bubbles percolating from time to time. You'll have to sit quietly and really study hard. After a while you should be able to determine a particular area where you might do some hunting and stalking. Get creative and design some kind of scoop and a stick to poke around or even sharpen a stick to a point and use a spearing technique. If you know how to weave, you can even attempt to make some kind of a net, but that will probably consume a lot of time. Better to wait for nightfall and hunt 'a'ama.

◈ *'Ōhiki*—This is the ghost crab or sand crab. This is the one that creates all those crab holes on the sandy beaches. Sit on the beach, wait for the crab to reveal itself out of its hole, then attack.
The crab will scamper across the sandy beach or go back in its hole. Your task is to chase it or dig deep at a rapid pace into its hole and catch it on its escape.

SEA URCHINS

The general Hawaiian word for sea urchin is *wana* (pronounced "vah-nah"). Wana have sharp and dangerous spines. It is a nasty poke and very painful, so when handling and harvesting, be very careful and watch where you step as well. Most people who are injured by wana step on them, especially surfers who wipeout and end up
standing on a reef barefoot. Fishermen and people who frequent the shoreline usually carry or wear *tabi*, reef walkers, rubber boots or beat up walking shoes to walk comfortably on these surfaces.

The species I am most familiar with are *'ina kea* (the white one), *'ina 'ula* (the red one) and *hawa'e* (the purple/black one). This last one is the standard spiny urchin locals usually mean when they refer to wana. These can be venomous, but they all hurt if you step on them, so harvest with a stick. Knock off the spines with a rock. Crush open the body. You can eat the five orange tongues and drink the liquid. The other sea urchin enjoyed by locals is the *ha'uke'uke*. This wana is the fat, big one with large spines that are not sharp but more flattened. Eat them the same way; the meat and liquid are delicious and full of nutritional value.

If stung by wana, treat similarly to jellyfish stings (see page 15). Use vinegar, lime juice or citric acid to soak the injury and dissolve the spines—they might not come out any other way.

HOW TO HARVEST ʻOPIHI

ʻOpihi is perhaps the most precious of the Hawaiian shoreline creatures that are harvested and eaten. My daughters call ʻopihi "gold." It is an acquired taste. This salty, briny creature is incredible when you put it on the grill and eat it like an oyster shooter with some *shoyu*, lemon and hot sauce! It is also served traditionally as a raw dish with all the juice inside, too.

ʻOpihi is of the limpet family. Because its taste is so valued in Hawaiʻi and it can be difficult to harvest, it is very expensive to purchase. It is often dangerous to harvest or pick ʻopihi because they choose to live under the surface of the water and cling to the top of shoreline rocks. Here, rocks are jagged, sharp and slippery, and wave and tide conditions are always in transition. Still, it is a favorite pastime and part of our lifestyle growing up in these islands. As always, your best bet is to go with somebody that knows how to pick ʻopihi. A person experienced in this adventure can tell you all the dos and don'ts. If you decide to go by yourself or with someone that is inexperienced, here are some tips:

◈ Never ever face your back to the ocean. Hawaiians say it is disrespectful to face your butt to the waves. Common sense, of course, is to face the ocean or periodically check so you can monitor the waves.

◈ It's best to go with a partner so you can watch out for each other. Sometimes one guy does the picking while one guy becomes the lookout.

- Another rule I live by and was taught by my kūpuna was a very simple phrase: "If you gotta watch waves, you shouldn't be picking 'opihi."

- Essential equipment list:
  - Tabi or reef shoes
  - Nylon net bag
  - Mask and snorkel
  - Palette knife or anything that can shuck the shells off the rocks

- If you are in a survival situation, you have to be creative:
  - Sharp stone
  - Pockets
  - Harvest only above the water

- Some basic protocol:
  - "No take anything quarter-size or smaller."
  - "No bolo head (make bald) the rock."
    Meaning, don't take all the 'opihi from that area.

- Three species of 'opihi:
  - *Ko'ele*—gray foot; the largest kind
  - *Alinalina*—yellow foot
  - *Makaiauli*—green border

If you're in a survival situation, 'opihi shells are good tools. You can make them into a good scaler for fish or scraper for all kinds of things. For non-survival uses, 'opihi shells also make nice jewelry.

HOW TO TRACK OCEAN FISH

The basics are simple: Learn to see the fish, to identify them and know their habits. But the art of seeing and tracking fish with the naked eye takes many years of training. Knowledge-building experience (*'ike* in Hawaiian), trial and error, and mentorship with a good teacher will improve your ability and skill. I have been blessed to be mentored by some great *lawai'a* (fishermen).

Where to look and what to look for:

◈ Start by getting a good pair of polarized sunglasses.

◈ Learn to spot shadows, ripples, moving or flipping tails and wakes in the water.

◈ Some big fish—and schools of smaller fish—are so large that they leave a noticeable wake on the surface.

◈ Fish like to hang out near fallen trees, pipelines, coral tables, rock shelves or piles in the water. To attract fish to net or spear, old-time fishermen would build a rock pile in the reef to create a haven, called a fishing *ko'a*, to attract near-shore fish.

On a sunny day with a calm ocean:

◈ Look for shadows in the water as you walk along the shoreline or climb the cliff of a fisherman's trail.

◈ Watch the waves as they crash onto the reef. As the waves build up before breaking, look for shadows moving in the lifting swell. You may even see fish surfing the waves.

On a cloudy, overcast day:

◈ When the sun is behind the clouds, the effect can create a gloomy light in the reflections of the water.

◈ Look for ripples and swirls that don't match the patterns of the rest of the water's surface.

HOW TO USE A THROW NET

A traditional fishing method adopted by the Hawaiians from the Japanese, throw-net fishing is an extremely effective way to catch multiple fish at one time. When you first attempt this task, you may feel confused and disoriented. This is a good exercise in training your brain to coordinate with your body to move in a different and unaccustomed way. Because of its complex nature, net throwing is a skill that's best learned from a teacher in person. If you'd like to try your hand at it on your own, here are a few pointers:

◈ Always make sure to hold the net so the weighted fishing leads hang straight down.

◈ We call the center of the net the *piko* (belly button). It's often marked with a loop wrapped in colored ribbon or tape.

◈ Many nets have an area near the edge where the netting bulges out. We call that the bag.

Here is the step-by-step procedure for preparing to throw the net:

1. Hold your net with your left hand and stretch the net length out with the leads down on the ground. Check and correct the net if it is twisted or tangled.

2. With your right hand, measure a big chest length from the top of the net. Then create a neat hold by folding the top of the net over once and then again. When you hold the net in your left fist at hip height, the leads should hang at about knee level. The net should look like a *hula* skirt and your right hand should be free at this point.

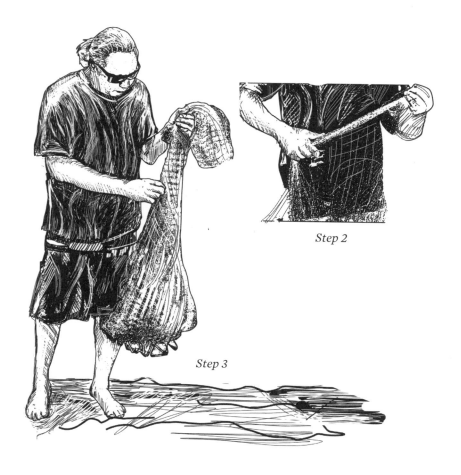

Step 2

Step 3

Step 4

3. Using the thumb and index finger of your right hand, pinch the netting at a point about halfway between your left hand and the leads. Using your middle three fingers in rhythm, like plucking a harp, gather about one-third of the net in your right hand. Here are some tips:

> ◇ Go slowly and methodically as you observe the lead and bottom of the net. The net should flow gracefully as you receive that first third into your right hand.

> ◇ Check that the net isn't tangling and the leads aren't twisted. If there is a twist or a tangle, shake it out, but don't use your hand to untangle.

4. This is the tricky part: Grab the third of the net that you just gathered with your right hand and move it across your body, under and around the outside of your left elbow and throw it up over your left shoulder or upper arm. (You can bring the netting up as high as your shoulder to help secure it, especially if you will be walking any distance with it before throwing.) Once the gathered portion of the net is resting comfortably on your arm, release your right hand. Now, one-third of the net is hanging over your left arm and the top of the net is held in your left hand. Your elbow should be behind the netting.

Step 5

5. Bend your right knee and turn it out to a 45-degree angle. With your right hand, grasp the lead on the outer edge of the remaining hanging part of the net and anchor it behind your knee. The leads on the edge of the net closest to your body should now be crossing your body from left hip to right upper thigh; those on the outside, away from your body, should be dangling around shin level. In a smooth, left-to-right motion, drape the folds of the net over your extended right knee. Continue gathering folds and anchoring them behind your knee until you have about one-third of the net draped around your knee.

6. After you have draped the second third of the net over your knee, rest it there for a bit. Your knee is still bent so the net should not slip.

7. Now, with your right hand, grab the final third of the net that's dangling in your left hand. Grasp it firmly about midway down (around thigh level) and bring it up to your left hand. Grab it below your right hand so that you now have the whole folded length in your left hand. (Remember you're still also holding the top of the net in your left hand—don't drop that!)

Step 8

8. With your right hand, grab the section of net resting on your knee while simultaneously grabbing the back lead edge. (Some people, like me, grasp the lead in their hand, anchoring it using the thumb.) You should now be holding the part of the net that was over your knee in your right hand.

9. Now is the time to check that the net appears to be open at the bottom. If you're grabbing the front lead or have missed any of the steps, the net will not appear open and will definitely not open when you throw it.

Throwing the net:

◈ In one smooth motion, throw the net out and downward. Do not throw it up into the air—there are no fish in the sky!

Pulling it in:

◈ Always make sure the leads are hanging down. Don't lift up the edge of the net—you'll let the fish escape and then all your hard work will be for nothing.

Throwing the Net

◈ If you cast the net over sandy ground, go for the piko. Gently pull the netting on top toward you until you can reach the center point. Grasp the piko and slowly pull upward. The leads will drag along the sandy bottom, meet together and trap the fish. Once the leads are clustered together, effectively closing the net with the fish inside, you can pull it out of the water. Don't forget to keep those leads hanging down toward the ground.

◈ If you cast the net over a rocky reef area, wrap each fish in the net surrounding it. Remember not to lift the edges! Bundle the fish, one at a time. If you attempt to pull the net in, the uneven ground will raise the edges and your fish will get away.

◈ As you pull in the net, the more you do to get those fish tangled up, the more likely you are to get them safely on shore. Remember: You haven't caught a fish until it's in the bucket.

HOW TO CLEAN A FISH

A s excellent fishermen and masters of many different fishing techniques, Hawaiians have always taught their *keiki* (children) how to clean a fish.

1. Scale your fish. Some don't need to be scaled but most require it. Use a spoon or an 'opihi shell—anything with an edge that allows you to scrape off the scales. Take your time and remove all the scales, even on the top of head and the underside. When you're eating a delicious piece of fish, nothing is worse than taking a bite with scales in it.

2. Remove the entrails and guts. Insert the tip of a knife into the anus and slit up to the gill area. You can go around one of the pelvic fins or cut right through the fins to the gills. Do not cut too deeply with the knife—you want to avoid accidentally cutting open the stomach and releasing its smelly contents.

3. Discard the innards. Stick your index finger into the gill area and slide the finger through to the other side of the fish that is holding the back of the connecting bone. Using a little elbow grease, simply yank out that whole section with gills intact. Pull all the way down to the original incision in the anus. Most or all of the innards should come out intact.

4. Rinse the fish thoroughly and scrape out any other excess blood and guts. Now it's ready for cooking.

CIGUATERA SAFETY

Ciguatera poisoning is a risk when consuming fish tainted with ciguatoxins, which colonize in coral beds. This means reef fish, which eat coral, are certainly a risk, as are any fish which may have eaten those fish. That's the food chain, yeah? You cannot detect ciguatera by sight, smell or taste. Most dangerously, it cannot be eliminated by cooking. The poison causes vomiting and diarrhea and can affect the nervous system, causing tingling sensations or making you feel hot and cold sensations in reverse. If you notice any of these symptoms and you recently ate your fresh catch, get medical attention immediately. All this isn't to say you can't safely consume what you catch. Commercial testing kits are available at fishing supply stores or online.

HOW TO DEAL WITH EELS

Eels live in holes and crevices in coral reefs and rock formations where other ocean residents, such as octopus, are also found. Hawai'i's many fish ponds (*loko i'a*), comprised of layers of rocks from the ocean floor to the surface, are also eel habitats. Here are a few tips on eel awareness:

AVOIDANCE AND SAFETY

◈ When you're out swimming, snorkeling or diving, watch where you put your hands and where your body is in relation to reefs and rocks. Pockets in these formations are often eel holes.

◈ Don't go swimming or wading if the water has been chummed or someone has cleaned fish in the area. Although generally shy, eels will come out of their holes to feed on the scraps. They will usually extend just a portion of their bodies out of the hole to grab the food. But if they're really hungry, they can become aggressive and come completely out of the hole for a feeding frenzy.

◈ Eels will bite to retrieve. A human's reaction to the bite is to pull away at the same moment. With both sides pulling in opposite directions, this makes for a nasty injury.

TREATMENT

◈ An eel's mouth carries plenty of bacteria, so be sure to clean even a surface bite very well. (For a deep bite, of course, seek medical attention immediately.) Use a first aid kit and bite down on a rolled-up T-shirt or whatever else is handy, because it will hurt big-time when the bite is cleaned out thoroughly with water, alcohol or other antiseptic.

◈ After cleaning, bandage the injury to stop the bleeding and hold the injured area above your heart. And make sure your tetanus shots are current.

HOW TO FIND AN OCTOPUS ON THE REEF

This is a great ocean skill, as it isn't easy to find a marine creature that can blend in with a reef and make itself look like a rock. The Hawaii an word for octopus is he'e. Hawai'i people also refer to it by its Japanese name, *tako*. Here's how to locate, hunt and harvest he'e.

Of course, you can seek out an experienced fisherman to guide you, but many local tako fishermen are very territorial about their special spots

Octopus is usually found inside the barrier reef in shallow water. Your terrain will be the shoreline floor and scattered sections of coral and rock formations called patch reefs.

What you will need:

⬦ A three-prong spear or a fairly long stick about a yard in length.

⬦ Nighttime: Light to no wind, low tide and a big, bright moon. Wear reef walkers to cross the reef and take along a mesh fish bag, a dive light or torchlight and a spear or stick.

⬦ Daytime: Clear sunny skies, variable winds, clear non-murky water in shallow reef sections, either low tide or high tide. You can either walk the reef areas or snorkel. Wear reef walkers, polarized sunglasses and a dive mask, and take with you a mesh fish bag, and a stick or spear.

What to do:

⬥ The objective is to find an octopus hiding or sleeping in reef holes. Be sure to check the holes with your spear or stick, not your hand.

⬥ When you find an octopus, use your stick or spear to tickle and agitate it until it grabs the spear and wraps its tentacles around it. Wait until you feel the octopus lock down, then pull it out of its reef hideaway.

⬥ Now comes the fun and adventure of peeling the octopus off the spear or stick and putting it into the mesh bag!

Who knows? You may get lucky, as I once did, and simply find one basking in the sun on the surface of a rock.

"ONE OF THE GREAT SKILLS YOU CAN
LEARN IN THE BUSH IS THE ABILITY TO
RECOGNIZE RESOURCES AND KNOW WHAT
YOU CAN USE IN AN ENVIRONMENT TO
BUILD OR CREATE."

LAND SKILLS

HOW TO WAYFIND IN THE HAWAIIAN FOREST

Wayfinding uses all your powers of observation and awareness. It is all about reading the signs around you. You are looking for tracks—not footprint tracks, necessarily, but what we call "sign tracks," the signals that are all around giving you information. Wayfinding is a kind of "spatial intelligence" that uses your gut feeling, your observations and some common sense.

Markers, or *kaha*, help you find your way:

◈ Look for obvious trail signs, like broken branches or marks carved on rocks or trees.

◈ Keep an eye out for things that don't belong. Sometimes, people leave subtle clues. Some of my family members planted lemon trees deep in the bush to signal to themselves where they were.

◈ Make your own markers in your mind. Identify a distinctive tree or rock, like the big rock that looks like a gorilla, to remember every turn.

Read the trees:

◈ If you see trees growing bent over, like how grass looks when the wind blows, you know that the wind comes that way often and pretty strong.

◈ You can compare the position of the sun (it rises in the east and sets in the west) to the direction the trees are bending to know the direction of the wind.

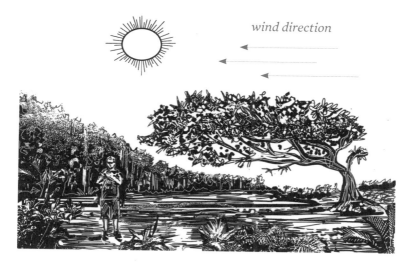

wind direction

◈ The mossy side of the tree is usually the side the rain comes from.

Things nibble on things:

◈ You can tell if there are animals around by seeing if there are bites taken out of leaves and fruits.

Plants reveal the terrain:

◈ *Maile* (a fragrant vine-like shrub) grows near cliffs. Tread carefully if you see or smell it.

◈ *Naupaka* (a shrub with distinctive half flowers) has two variants; one grows on the beach and one grows in the mountains. Combined with your other senses and observations, you'll know which way you're heading if you spot it.

- Lush, green plants can be a sign that you are over a water table.

- *Hapuʻu* (tree ferns) and other kinds of ferns like to grow near water.

HOW TO DEAL WITH BEING LOST

I f you think you are lost, then you are. There are a few things you can—and should—do BEFORE you head out into the bush or to the ocean to make life a little safer and easier in the event that you do get lost:

◈ Plan a time frame for your outing, an approximation of how long you plan to be in the bush. Will it be an all-day trip, overnight excursion or a three-day camp?

◈ Tell someone where you are going before you begin your field trip. This should be done every time you go out for a camping trip or an outdoor adventure. Some of the worst calamities happen because of failure to do this simple task.

◈ Be sure to travel with appropriate emergency gear and be prepared for an unexpected overnighter with warm and waterproof gear. Have a flashlight, knife, matches and water. For the ocean, have fins and/or tabi.

◈ Know where the main and frequently traveled trails and dirt roads are in the area.

Try NOT to get lost, of course. Here are some tips as you start out into the wilderness:

◈ Orient yourself with your starting point. Familiarize yourself with the surroundings. Know where the four directions (north, south, east, west) are in relation to your starting point.

◈ Not every trail is marked, especially "bushee-bush" (off the beaten trail). Define your own "mental markers." Look for a recognizable type of plant, a distinctly shaped tree or rock, and fix its shape, size and color in your mind. Remember what to do when you see it (turn left or right, head uphill or down, etc.).

◈ If you lack confidence, lay a trail with physical marks (this is called "blazing"): bend branches, carve and make a mark on a succession of trees or rocks.

◈ Always pay attention to the time of day. If you can't see where you're going, you're gonna get lost.

If you do get lost (or maybe you're just disoriented), keep calm and don't forget to be mindful. Keep your eyes and ears open. Outdoors, your awareness of your surroundings and observational skills can become a built-in compass and clock. And remember, safety first. You don't want to be lost AND hurt.

◈ Get your bearings. Figure out what direction you're going.

  ◇ Look for the position of the sun.

  ◇ Be aware of the wind direction.

  ◇ Look at the movement of the clouds.

◈ If you're lost at sea, observe ocean tides, watch currents and wave patterns, notice reefs and channels.

◈ Know your *mauka* (toward the mountain) and *makai* (toward the ocean). Use those directions to guide you.

  ◇ Find and follow a river bed. It will eventually lead to the shoreline.

  ◇ Listen for the sound of the ocean.

  ◇ Look for a clearing where you can see where the mountains and the sea are.

  ◇ On an island, if you get high up enough, you will always be able to spot the ocean. Climb up to a high vantage point or cliffside so you can look for the sea.

  ◇ Follow the animals; they are creatures of habit. They like to go up and down through gulches, mauka to makai.

◈ Locate and remember landmarks; mark your trail if unfamiliar with area. This way, you'll know if you're wandering in circles.

◈ See the previous section for more wayfinding tips.

◈ Know and use emergency signals to seek help.

HOW TO AVOID OR SURVIVE
A FLASH FLOOD

Hawai'i has two seasons: *ho'oilo* (wet season) and *wela* (dry or hot season). Especially during the former, be prepared for wet weather, rainstorms and flash floods whenever you're hiking in the rainforest. A trickling stream can very quickly become a raging torrent when the rain is pouring farther up mauka.

PREVENTION

- ◈ Always check the weather report before heading into the rainforest.

- ◈ Always tell someone where you're going, even if you have to leave a written note or phone message. Make this mandatory; it's only common sense.

- ◈ Always make sure you know where you're going and that you've got your bearings right. What's the name of trail you're walking or hiking on? Which way are you heading for your destination? What level of physical conditioning do you need for the trek?

- ◈ Make sure you have proper rain gear: enough protection to hunker down in case of an emergency or flash flood.

- ◈ Especially on overnight trips, it's a good idea to take some rope along.

SURVIVAL

◈ If you should run into a flash flood situation, head for higher ground immediately. You might even find yourself climbing a tree to get out of harm's way.

◈ Stay out of low-lying areas such as gulches, riverbeds, etc.

◈ The worst case scenario is to use that rope you brought to hoist or tie down your body, or to rappel or swing to safety.

◈ Once you escape to higher ground, just wait it out. Eventually, the water will slow down and recede. Being calm, comfortable and confident with the natural world is key. It's better to spend an uncomfortable, but comparatively safe, night outside than to try to cross back over flash flood waters and be swept away or hurt.

HOW TO TREAT A BLISTER

T he ancient Hawaiians went barefoot, and I have a few friends with leather-like soles who can walk through all sorts of terrain. For most of us who trek outdoors, however, good walking shoes are a must. Trouble is, even good shoes can cause blisters, especially when they're new.

PREVENTION

◈ Buy shoes that fit right, of course—not too loose so the foot rubs back and forth, creating friction from the space in between; not too tight, which can cause rubbing and sweating because the foot has no room to breathe. Bring the socks you plan to wear to the fitting. Break them in with training well before you head for the hills.

◈ Consider a well-worn, but still hardy, pair of athletic shoes or boots that are already broken-in.

◈ Use cotton and wool socks to provide comfort and cushioning. Sometimes, wearing double socks can help cushion the feet, but be mindful of how this affects the fit of the shoes.

TREATMENT

◈ First, clean the blister by washing the area with soap and water, if available. If you are in an area with ʻawapuhi (ginger blossom), these plants retain water and can be used in place of an antiseptic to create a natural and soothing soap or shampoo. If none are available, use a clean cloth and wipe the surface carefully to avoid breaking the blister.

◈ Next, use heat to sterilize a needle or a knifepoint. Prick the edge of the unbroken blister and drain the fluid.

◈ Do not remove the blistered skin; you will need it for protection. Cover the blister with an adhesive bandage that covers an area beyond the blister itself.

◈ If you have no first aid kit, look for laukahi leaves (see page 136) or an aloe plant (apply the sap to the affected area), or just clean the area with water from your canteen, then cut a part of your clothing to wrap.

HOW TO HANDLE DIFFICULT TERRAIN

Tracking and trekking in Hawai'i often involves a lot of climbing, together with what I call SWIG—"somewhat intelligent guessing." In general, you can keep out of trouble this way:

◈ Have a good, sturdy pair of hiking shoes.

◈ Always look ahead on the trail so you know what you are dealing with.

◈ Plan your strategy *vis-a-vis* terrain and weather ahead of time.

◈ Approach each trek with confidence and focus.

◈ On Hawai'i's steep ridges and valley walls, sometimes going up and coming down is accomplished in one main position—on your butt.

◈ To ascend or descend safely in forested areas, you might have to grab and go from tree to tree.

◈ When reaching for a tree, bush or rock, look before you grab and make sure that it is safe, strong and steady and can handle your weight. Many Island bushes and plants have thorns, and rocks in Hawai'i's always-eroding mountain areas can be slippery and loose.

◈ When going around switchbacks and turnarounds, "Hug da mountain"—always lean the majority of your body weight towards the mountain.

◈ On a tight trail, try to not look below, especially if you fear heights. Focus on *pili* (sticking) to the mountain. Keep either your chest or your butt and back facing the mountain. Move slow, one step at a time, one foot at a time.

HOW TO BE SAFE ON THE LAVA FIELDS

The Hawai'i Island volcanic area is one of the most active cauldrons in the world. This is a place where the Earth Mother gives birth to the life of the land. You will never experience anything quite like this. It is a natural show that has been happening since the beginning of time. The Big Island of Hawai'i is the only island in the Hawaiian chain with active volcanoes. Access near the flow area is highly regulated for the sake of visitor safety. Information on adventure treks, state laws and regulations regarding volcano area visits is readily available online. For the most up-to-date information on active sites and area closures, visit the Hawai'i Volcanoes National Park website (www.nps.gov/havo).

◈ The most important thing about lava flow exploring is: Don't get lost!

◈ Never travel by yourself. Lava flows are something you don't tangle with alone. Go with a friend or tour group.

◈ Wear protective clothing. A good pair of walking or hiking shoes is a must. The thicker the soles, the smaller the chance of burning your feet in case you walk in a recent flow area. Most ground cover in a recent flow area is extremely hot and lava is probably still flowing beneath the surface.

◈ If you have respiratory illnesses it is absolutely not a good idea to visit a lava flow due to the "vog" (volcanic smog), which contains sulfur gases. It is dangerous for anyone to breathe that tainted air too long and at close range.

◈ Before entering the field, have your "common sense eyes and ears" on point. Turn on your inner compass and keep your peripheral vision aware of your surroundings. This is a lava flow—it is dangerous.

◈ There are designated trails marked for visitors. Never go off the beaten trail without a guide or permission. It is very easy to get disoriented within a lava field because black lava fields all look the same. Make sure you know your sense of direction, north-south-east-west or mauka-makai (see pages 52-57).

◈ Be mindful. It's easy to get distracted by one of Mother Nature's greatest spectacles.

  ◇ Always look up at the sky to see which way the clouds are moving. Which way is the wind blowing?

  ◇ Where is my shadow? Where is the sun?

◈ Keep an eye out for steam vents. These are places where ground water seeps down to the hot rocks below and comes up as steam. These can be dangerous because the steam itself is quite hot and also because they signal a place where there is a puka in the ground. In addition to the rising steam, volcanic gases may be coming up, another reason to treat them with care.

◈ Before entering, silently ask permission and pay respects to this sacred place. Offer reverence and respect to our Madame Pele, the Goddess of Fire. She is the most powerful of all the gods and deities in Hawaiian culture. She is said to roam the countryside from time to time taking the form of a human—a beautiful maiden or an elderly woman with long white hair.

◈ Never remove lava rocks. It is said that if a rock is taken, it can cause calamities and misfortune for as long as one holds that rock. Many stories have been told about people having to travel back to Hawaiʻi Island to replace the rock in the same area along with an offering of apology. From a more practical standpoint, disturbing rocks, plants and artifacts is bad for the natural ecosystem.

HOW TO MAKE USE OF NATIVE PLANTS

Hawaiian plants have all kinds of uses. Here are four that are common and can be used to do all kinds of things in survival and non-survival situations. When harvesting from trees, do it correctly. The phrase to remember is "No bolo head the tree." That means don't harvest so much off one plant that it looks like someone has given it a haircut ("bolo head" = bald). Also, when picking leaves, pull from the stem and make a clean pull off the main plant.

KALO

Most of the world today is familiar with poi, the gooey paste that is eaten with fingers at a Hawaiian *lū'au*. Poi derives from *kalo*, the taro plant and the most valuable food plant of the Hawaiian people. As the primary staple food since ancient times, several varieties of kalo were brought to the islands by  different Polynesian and South Pacific groups. In time, all islands displayed terraces of planted taro. Through crossbreeding and reproduction, it is said that there are now more than two hundred different species of kalo in existence. Kalo is Hawai'i.

◈ Eating—An underground root about the size of a potato, kalo is mainly used for eating.

　◇ Be careful: Do *not* eat kalo raw. Your tongue, throat and mouth will become tremendously irritated from the crystals released from the calcium oxalate contained in the corm.

◇ Steaming, baking and boiling kalo are the usual and most popular methods of cooking.

◇ Cooked kalo can also be eaten in small chunks cut into the size of stew meat or pounded into a rough paste called *paʻi ai*.

◇ And of course, it can be eaten as poi by adding more water and kneading it until it is smooth.

◈ Artwork—Dyes were created to print designs from the cut ends of the stem. Hawaiians also used poi like rubber cement to stick two light and thin things together.

◈ First aid—Cut a section of the kalo leaf stem and apply the sap to a cut to stop the bleeding.

NIU

Among the top native plants on my list for survival is the *niu* or coconut palm, one of the most important and versatile plants used by Hawaiians. Here are some of the many uses derived from parts of this precious tree:

◈ Fronds can be used to:
  ◇ Thatch roofs and build a number of different shelters
  ◇ Make a hat for sun and rain protection
  ◇ Make a torchlight holder

◈ Husk fibers can be used to:
  ◇ Make fire by using it as tinder
  ◇ Make cordage (see page 73 for more details)

◈ Shells can be:
  ◇ Used as a bowl or cup
  ◇ Carved into eating utensils

◈ Water and soft white meat:
  ◇ The original Gatorade, coconut water is an excellent source of hydration
  ◇ The edible white meat is very tasty and filling
  ◇ Both the water and the meat are used in traditional natural remedies for asthma, bladder and kidney problems and more

◈ The base of the tree trunk can be made into a stool, bed table or traditional Hawaiian drum.

◈ *'A'a niu*, the fabric-like material found where the fronds sprout from the tree trunk, makes for good matting to lay on the ground or even a carrier for a tinder bundle to make a fire (see page 113).

HAU

Easy to identify by its leaves, which are heart-shaped with a smooth upper surface and furry under surface, *hau* is a tree in the hibiscus family that mostly grows near the sea but can be found in many mountainous areas today. Like a vine, its crooked trunk has long tall branches that bend and weave  or shoot straight up to the sun and sky. Here are some of its uses:

◈ Fire—Rubbing two hau sticks together causing friction is the ancient Hawaiian (*ka poe kahiko*) way to make fire. It is the secret of fire (see page 113).

◈ Floaters—When dried, hau sticks are very light but durable, and make good floaters for outrigger canoe gear, nets and other fishing equipment.

◈ Cordage—Use the inner bark by stripping it (see page 73).

◈ Laxative—The sap found in the stems, flower buds and ovaries can be chewed and swallowed to treat constipation.

◈ Dry throat—Chew the young leaf buds of the hau until mashed up and then swallow to soothe a parched throat.

◈ The Hawaiians say hau can be also used for labor pains, chest congestion and more.

KI (OR TI)

Lā'ī is the traditional name for the ti leaf and in both ancient and modern times it is a symbol of *mana* (power) and connected to the god Lono. Many families had lā'ī on their properties believing that it warded off evil spirits. This plant has so many uses:

◈ Run some water on a leaf and put on your head—it cools you off!

◈ You can make a variety of lei using ti leaves.

◈ Hula dancers make hula skirts out of the leaves, acknowledging the Hawaiian goddess Laka.

◈ Spread out a whole bunch of leaves and use as a tablecloth at lū'au or parties.

◈ Use the young ti leaf to make a whistle. Cut the leaf in half (across the width) and roll the half without the stem into a trumpet-like shape. Blow.

◈ Wrap all kinds of things. To wrap something, you must make a slit in the leaf spine and peel the rigid spine away from the leaf so you have a flexible piece to use like fabric.

◇ Wrap a leaf around your head or place on your forehead to relieve a headache or fever.

⬧ Wrap gifts or *hoʻokupu* (offerings).

⬧ Wrap *laulau*—a Hawaiian dish steamed with lūʻau leaves and pork, chicken and butterfish—or if you are in survival-mode, you can wrap whatever food you have on hand to cook it.

◈ Make a netted frame and tie and layer leaves to make a raincoat.

◈ Make Hawaiian sandals or slippers (flip-flops) from leaves by weaving, layering and braiding them together.

◈ Tie leaves on the top of your surround net to scare fish and keep them in the net.

◈ Smash the roots of the plant and make *ʻōkolehao* (Hawaiian moonshine).

HOW TO MAKE CORDAGE

Rope is an essential survival item. If you're planning on spending the night in the bush or on the shore, you should make sure to take some. But if you run into a situation where you need to tie some stuff together, knowing how to make cordage is a good skill. You won't be able to climb down a mountain with either of these, but you can at least keep things from flying away or hold them together.

HAU

Cordage made from hau is sturdy. It's more like rope, or you can just use single strips to bind things, too.

1. Strip the bark from hau branches.
2. Soak in water until the strips are soft and pliable.
3. Braid to make strong rope or use single strips to bind things together.
4. Let dry.

NIU

Coconut fiber cordage is skinnier than the kind you make with hau—it's more like twine. You can also use the fronds the same way you use hau: Braid them together to make a stronger length.

1. Strip the fibers from inside a green coconut.
2. Roll a small bunch of fibers together between your palms; this will be your first strand.
3. Repeat the process so you have two or three strands.
4. Braid or twine your strands together.

HOW TO POOP IN THE WOODS

Everyone knows the sayings: "When you gotta go, you gotta go," "Everybody poops." There's no time to be shy when it comes to taking a poo in the woods. The worst thing you can do is hold it. You will eventually get sicker. Just let it flow.

The basics of going to the bathroom in the bush:

◈ Grab some toilet tissue if you have it.

◈ Get off the main trail.

◈ Stay out of the wind direction with respect to others you may be cruising with.

◈ Pay attention to prickly plants like cactus or *kiawe*. We don't have poison ivy in Hawai'i, but many plants that ooze sap can make you itchy, too.

◈ Look out for bugs and spiderwebs.

◈ Dig a small hole and assume the position (squat like a sumo wrestler).

◈ Sometimes you don't even need to dig a hole, just do your business and then cover with rocks or leaves.

Did you know that if you forget to bring toilet paper when you go into the bush that using the T-shirt off your back is an option? Always start off with your sleeves—tear them off and use as needed. You will walk out of the bush with a new tank top, but at least your insides won't be all clenched up.

Other items you can use if you didn't remember the TP:

⬦ Smooth leaves (make sure they don't have rough fibers)—ti, banana and ginger are good ones

⬦ Crumpled paper—crumpling it up and smoothing it out several times makes it softer

⬦ Your shirt or other sacrificeable items of clothing are always best since you know they won't be scratchy or make you itchy

HOW TO DEVELOP THE EYE OF THE TRACKER

When you are out and about in the natural world, whether on a leisurely hike or a hardy trek into the wilderness, it is wise to pay attention to what surrounds you and to have your senses on full alert. Tracking is a primal skill for human beings that also helps us develop our vision. John Stokes, one of my own tracking teachers, put it best: "Tracking lets you follow something—the track of an animal, a person, a memory, a concept—with all your senses as far as you can. It's the process of bonding your energy with the energy of that something or someone you're following." Here are the two requirements for developing the "eye of the tracker":

◈ Peripheral vision incorporates the full extension and capabilities of your eyesight. Some call this wide-angle vision, full-court vision or open-field vision. Trackers call it "soft eyes." When outdoors, look out and take in the full landscape or seascape in front of you. Notice all movements and then focus on and isolate certain movements.

◈ Varied vision is the ability to see things at a great distance, as far as your eyes can see, and then to adjust, in seconds, right back to the tip of your nose. Think of it as similar to adjusting binoculars for a long-distance look and then looking right back in front of you through a magnifying glass. The tracker trains at being able to shift back and forth very quickly, so as not to miss anything in a constant wave of rhythmic observation.

HOW TO READ ANIMAL TRACKS

By following tracks and reading them, a tracker is able to tell an animal's story from the moment of observing the first track until the unsuspecting animal is found. Local people will say, "Try see if you can find 'um, before it find you." It takes many years to be considered "accomplished" in the art of tracking. Just as in music, to become good you have to pay your dues; to become a good tracker you must do your "dirt time."

Tracking is like a CSI investigation. It teaches you to observe and make intelligent guesses about what has happened, what's going to happen next and eventually discovering, finding and completing the story. It is so much fun—it stimulates your imagination and creativity, and increases your observation and awareness skills. It really teaches you how to be mindful in so many ways, including your physical movements and your innate intuitions.

Here's a starter kit of notes that you can practice as you take that walk into the bush on your first tracking adventure.

◈ Before you go, study up on how to identify different animal tracks. Observe the difference between the front foot and the back foot. Deer and pig are good ones to start with since they are so common in Hawai'i.

◈ Out in the bush, find a series or set of tracks that you can follow. Notice the size, the shape, the depth of the track. This is the first step in determining the size and weight of the animal and the differentiation and isolation of this animal track from another.

◈ Find another set of tracks so you can start to make observations and comparisons.

◈ Use popsicle sticks as markers to measure out a set of tracks. Mark the heel of the track or the digit (toe) of the track. Toe or heel, just remember to keep that consistent. Place the popsicle stick on the outer edge of the track. This will eventually teach you to read the width of the creature and cool stuff like if it is a female or male, if it is a female who has given birth, etc.

◈ Use "The Twelve" exercise to practice your observation skills. Start with a set of twelve tracks. Think of them like musical notes on a staff. After planting popsicle sticks on your twelve tracks, step back and take a wider view of your "phrase." It looks like a musical melody. Now you can start to study the song and tell the story. You will learn through trial and error that these footprints and signs occur very naturally. You will start to piece it together, build your story and visualize accurately what this animal looks like, what it was doing and where was it going.

◈ After practicing a bit, see how far you can follow a set of tracks. Every so often, glance up to see what's ahead. Sometimes with a little skill and quietness—oh, and a bit of luck—you might run right into the critter up ahead.

◈ Remember: Tracking is fun. Tracking is very cool. Tracking keeps you on point.

"TRACKING TEACHES YOU TO OBSERVE
AND MAKE INTELLIGENT GUESSES
ABOUT WHAT HAS HAPPENED,
WHAT'S GOING TO HAPPEN NEXT AND
EVENTUALLY DISCOVERING, FINDING
AND COMPLETING THE STORY."

HOW TO AVOID A WILD PIG ATTACK

If you are hiking on a designated trail in Hawai'i, you'll often see wild pig tracks. Hawai'i's pig population is overabundant, very healthy and about as crowded as traffic in Honolulu. If you wander off the beaten path, you're even more likely to come face-to-face with a wild pig. Here's how to spot and avoid them:

- ◈ If you see lots of tracks and evidence of digging, stay on the main trail. Pigs like to eat roots and wallow in muddy areas of the rainforest.

- ◈ Keep your head up and watch what's ahead on the trail. Sometimes you will see the pigs before they see you— sometimes.

- ◈ While walking on a trail, look left to right to spot cross trails made by pigs. These are animal runs. Sometimes you meet a pig at one of the crossroads.

- ◈ Mud rubbings are another indication of pig activity. Pigs like to rub their bodies against tree trunks and leave mud rubbings behind in doing so. These rubbings can show you the size of the pig and how recently or long ago the animal was in the area.

- ◈ If confronted or startled by a pig barreling down a pig run or main trail, jump aside and get onto or behind a tree to avoid a charge.

- ◈ A charging pig is an angry pig. He will come at you and try to bite or gouge you with his tusks. These animals are fast and agile. Get off that trail the pig thinks he owns.

HOW TO HUNT WILD PIG

As mentioned before, Hawai'i's wild pig population throughout the state is overwhelming. There are so many running amok, hunting season is open year-round. It is quite a rush to encounter a wild pig in the rainforest. Even if you're intentionally tracking or hunting them, you should know how to avoid them—see page 73 for that and tips on how to spot the signs of one.

If you want to hunt pig, there are many locals that hunt on every island, and like I always say, it's "da best" to go with someone who knows what he's doing. A professional guide or a local hunter will be familiar with the hunting area. Find one who follows the hunting code of ethics and has his Hawai'i Hunting License.

◈ A pig hunt is a highly intense adrenaline rush. It is a good idea to be prepared and in good shape for pig hunting. You will have to run and chase in adverse rainforest conditions over slippery, rocky, uneven terrain. And it is usually running up the mountain.

◈ You will need, at minimum: rope, a backpack, a hunting gun and/or a knife. For pig hunting, a long bayonet-type of knife is used. It's best to have at least three or four guys when you go out.

HUNTING WITH DOGS

◈ Most pig hunts in Hawai'i involve running dogs. The dogs do the actual work to track down the pigs and when they corner one, they will start to bark. The hunter just has to wait and listen good. Listen for the direction of the sound

of the bark. That gives you an idea of where the c
pig are and how far away.

◈ If you hear an occasional bark as they are tracking, the dogs
are on a wild boar (male). With a boar, the dogs' pursuit
will eventually aggravate him and he will turn around
to defend or fight. When he does this, the dogs will bark
constantly, what hunters call a "steady bark." If the dogs
find a sow (female) they will usually attack the sow and
grab it which will make the pig squeal. This how you can
tell the difference if your dogs have bayed a boar or a sow.

◈ When you hear the steady bark or the squeal, that is an
indication that the pig is surrounded. Hunters have to
pursue quickly and find their dogs before their dogs get
cut up by the tusks or bitten by the pig. You should know,
sometimes some dogs don't make it, but you must remember
that that is what they were bred for.

◈ When a pig is cornered, you will have to pull off the dogs and
tie them down while another hunter shoots or stabs the pig.
The best way to do this is to have someone grab and pull one
of the back legs of the pig. This puts the pig off balance and
causes it to fall. Then someone else must step in and stab an
incision behind the front leg of the animal poking towards
the middle to pierce the heart. If you are shooting the pig,
it should be a head shot or shot placement should be right
behind the ear. That way the bullet will enter the brain for an
ethical kill.

HUNTING WITHOUT DOGS

◈ Without dogs, you either need to do the tracking work or sit quietly on an active trail and wait for a pig to come by.

◈ Trapping is also an option, but it is a very complex process and it is better to learn it in person from someone.

AFTER THE HUNT

◈ Once you've killed the pig, you need to field dress it. See page 96 for instructions.

◈ After the basic field dressing, you can pack it out of the bush over your shoulders or on a pole, if you like to look rugged.

◈ Us older (and wiser!) guys prefer to skin, debone and cut up the meat to make it easier and lighter to carry.

 ◇ If you can't take everything, the best parts to pack out are the front shoulders, "hinds" (the hindquarters), "back strap" (along the spine), ribs, loin and brisket.

 ◇ When skinning and deboning pig meat, you WANT to keep as much fat on as possible. Fat is what makes the pig taste good. You know, BACON!

 ◇ As you debone the meat, hang it from trees or over bushes to give it a chance to cool down. (Make sure someone is on fly-chasing duty.)

◇ When you're ready to pack the meat out, wrap it in old pillowcases or burlap sacks before you put it in your backpack. Don't use plastic to wrap it up because it's not good for all that still-hot meat.

HOW TO TRACK AXIS DEER

The art of tracking deer is a skill taken seriously by hunters and trackers. Modern hunters are out to kill—harvest is a better word—deer primarily for trophies and sometimes for food. Trackers, on the other hand, are in pursuit of deer to hone and train their nature awareness skills. The tracker's success is measured by his or her ability to find the deer and get up as close as possible to the animal.

Here are a handful of basics to get you tracking some deer. Let's start with a few facts.

◈ Hawai'i is populated by axis deer, a spotted deer (even in maturity) which is a totally different beast from the whitetail, blacktail and mule deer found throughout North America. This species originates from Southeast Asia, primarily India. Also known as chital, these deer were given as a gift from Hong Kong to King Kamehameha V and were ordered by the king to be shipped from O'ahu and set free to roam on the island of Moloka'i, one of his favorite places to relax. Eventually, deer swam or were transported over to the other islands of the chain.

◈ There are no deer on the island of O'ahu, so to do some tracking, you will have to take a flight to our outer islands. The island most known for its deer is Moloka'i. Next in line with a bountiful deer population would be the island of Lāna'i, although in recent years the island of Maui has been the hot spot with an incredible increase of wild axis deer and a number of opportunities to observe them or even book a deer hunt. There are conflicting stories of deer sightings on the island of Hawai'i but at this time the population is minimal. The island of Kaua'i has a very unique and small herd of blacktail deer roaming Waimea Canyon and the private property of the Robinson family. Local people who have access and permission frequent the private property and the state land but it is a very hardy hike, so you will need to be in great shape to take on that adventure.

PREPARATION AND TRACKING

◈ Deer have an incredible sense of smell—really, they smell five times better than you. So, to increase your chances at tracking a deer in the bush, you should prepare a day ahead by not using any deodorant, cologne, perfume, body wash, shampoo, anything scented on the body. Don't even brush your teeth with toothpaste. Deer can smell toothpaste from a great distance.

◈ Camouflage clothing and outdoor hunting wear increase your chances of not being seen. Deer have incredible eyesight and can see objects moving from far away so you must blend in with the environment.

◈ Learn how to stalk. Practice moving slowly and quietly through the bush. Be light-footed and contort your body to look less like a human. Believe me, deer learn at a young age how to recognize a human. We trackers say when we talk about disguising ourselves, "Make like a tree."

◈ It is always a good idea to go with a guide, someone who knows the area so you don't get lost or trespass in an area you shouldn't be in. Sometimes landowners aren't very hospitable when they see visitors near or on their property. Get permission.

◈ Before you go, identify what a deer track looks like. Observe the difference between the front foot and the back foot.

◈ Axis deer usually travel in herds from groups of four to sometimes several hundred. With so many tracks, it can get confusing. Make sure you can isolate your series of tracks and that you are following the same animal.

◈ See pages 76-78 for more tracking tips.

HOW TO USE A RABBIT STICK

A rabbit stick, or throwing stick, is a primal, aboriginal way of harvesting fowl and small game. It's a very simple hunting tool, but quite challenging to master an accurate and strong throw for maximum impact.

What to look for:

◈ Find a stick that's heavier at one end and fits well in your hand.

◈ Try different lengths and sizes, but make sure the wood is solid and can perform the task. For example, I have a long rabbit stick made of a guava tree branch and a medium stout one made of kiawe (algaroba).

◈ If you're searching among deadfall wood, make sure the stick you pick isn't moist, waterlogged or home to small creatures.

◈ Once you've selected a solid deadfall stick or a length of living wood, saw it down to your desired length. Visualize the impact it will make on a good throw. Feel its balance and weight.

Throwing the stick:

◈ Take note of how far you can make an accurate throw.

◈ Throwing a rabbit stick is similar to skipping rocks across the water—a side throw from the hip. If you are close enough to your target, throw the stick directly.

◈ If your game is at a distance of fifteen to twenty yards, skip your throw so that it bounces off of the ground to tumble your prey, slowing or disabling it.

◈ If your game is farther away and you cannot stalk any closer, use an overhand or overhead throw to reach a longer distance.

HOW TO FIELD DRESS SMALL FOWL

Hawai'i has plenty of small game like pheasant and quail. If you can catch 'em with your rabbit stick, you can eat 'em! Concentrate on harvesting the breast meat. Here's how:

1. Lay the bird on the ground on its back, with its feet towards you and its head facing away.

2. Spread the wings out and step on them with both feet, as close as you can to its body, bracing the bird firmly on the ground.

3. Grab its legs and hold them firmly. Now pull and feel its body lift as it pulls away from the outer layer of feathers and skin.

4. Discard the waste and anything else you don't want from the bird, leaving just the breast section of both sides. Separate that as well and you have pan-sized breast pieces to cook.

HOW TO CATCH AND FIELD DRESS A CHICKEN

Wild chickens are fairly common in Hawai'i. As one of the staple and sustainable foods of our local culture, chicken is tasty, abundant and found throughout the Islands. Here's how to hunt and field dress a wild *moa* (in Hawaiian) or *manok* (in Filipino).

1. Stalk a wild chicken ever so slowly if you are using a throw net. When you are in range, throw ahead of the chicken for the net to cover distance and depth. The chicken will be caught in the middle of the net.

2. If you are using the rabbit stick (see page 90), you may not need to stalk as closely. But you must make an accurate and powerful enough throw to startle and tumble the chicken. Then grab that chicken quickly (if you haven't already killed it with the stick).

3. If the chicken is still alive, you must put it down. The quick and humane way is to grab its legs (be mindful of its leg spurs to avoid injury) and hold it upside down. This calms the chicken. Then swing the bird around several times to break its neck.

4. Immediately use your knife to slit its throat to drain the blood.

5. Field dressing a wild chicken is the same as dressing any other small fowl: Step on its wings and pull on its legs to lift the inner carcass right out of the skin and feathers.

HOW TO FIELD DRESS A DUCK

There are several species of wild ducks in the Islands, most of which graze and fly in sanctuaries and other protected areas. But once in a while, you'll come across a flock in the wild or a straggler or two cruising in an open swamp or pond. Here's a good way to harvest their tasty breast meat:

1. Hold the duck pressed against your chest, with its head up and to the side.

2. Place your hands around its chest cavity and use your fingers to feel and locate the center breast bone.

3. Now, massage your fingers into the bone until you feel the inner cavity.

4. Remove its coat of feathers and skin to reveal the breast meat area. (You can tear right through the thin skin.)

5. Now place the bird on the ground, laying it on its back sideways and facing you. Place one of your feet on its neck and head and the other on its legs.

6. Bend over and feel for the breast section with your fingers. Feel around inside the breast area. Secure a good hold and remove the breast meat section. Wings will also come up and out.

7. Simply cut off the wings and any other excess. The breast area should be clean and ready to be seasoned and cooked.

HOW TO FIELD DRESS A TURKEY

Wild turkeys roam throughout Hawai'i, especially on Moloka'i and the Big Island. Free-range turkeys are hardy, strong and hard-bodied fowl. Legs and all other meat are minimal and tough to eat. As with other wild game birds, go for the breast. Here's a simple technique for cleaning and cooking your gobbler caught in the wild:

1. Lay the bird on its back, legs facing you, head out in front, and spread the wings out and behind your legs. Watch out for the sharp spurs on the turkey's legs.

2. Pluck feathers from the breast area in a jerking motion in the direction of the head. Plucking is optional, but your dressing task is easier if you expose the skin and breast bone. It will also prevent feathers from getting on the meat when you open up the chest area.

3. Slit the skin with a sharp knife along the breast bone and carefully pull back the skin away from the meat.

4. Make an incision along the breast bone and slice the meat out on both sides of the center bone by gently peeling the breast piece off one side. Repeat the process on the other side.

5. Discard the rest of the fowl carcass, unless you want to keep the spurs and beard for a hunting trophy. Yield: Two nice pieces of turkey breast for the campfire.

HOW TO FIELD DRESS A WILD ANIMAL

The wild game we hunt in Hawai'i includes pigs, deer, sheep and goats. They may vary in size and shape, but the basics of field dressing are the same for removing the *na'au* (intestines, internal organs) from the animal. The main reasons for field dressing game are to lighten the load you carry and to prep the game to be quartered or deboned. This is a skill that everyone should try at least once, to develop self-confidence in the wild.

1. Make sure your knife is sharp and your hand is steady. Make an incision into the belly and cut all the way down to the anus. If it is a buck or a boar, remove the genitals. Be careful to cut around, not through, the genitals to remove them intact and completely. If water for cleansing is not readily available, before you begin the removal, squeeze the penis area to empty out any urine.

2. Next, cut around the rim of the anus, using a circle cut, and remove the organ inside.

3. Cut and trim away the legs. Then move up to the belly and make a very careful incision to avoid puncturing any internal organs, especially the stomach and intestines. Take the incision all the way up the sternum.

4. Insert your index and middle fingers to serve as a guide between the organs and the back of the knife as you cut up to the chest bone.

5. The internal organs will start to roll out of the body cavity. Now, put your hands inside the body cavity and pull the

rectum through. Stick your knife inside and cut here and there to loosen the diaphragm. Then pull this out; it will take some elbow grease.

6. With your knife, carefully reach deep into the neck of the animal. Feel for the windpipe and cut it.

7. With some extra cutting and trimming here and there, keep loosening and removing the internal organs until you pull out all the insides. Drain the blood.

"WHEN YOU ARE OUT AND ABOUT IN THE NATURAL WORLD, IT IS WISE TO PAY ATTENTION TO WHAT SURROUNDS YOU AND TO HAVE YOUR SENSES ON FULL ALERT."

GENERAL SKILLS & SAFETY

"In Hawai'i, we have two seasons: *kau wela* (dry) and *ho'oilo* (wet). Sun and rain, so simple!"

HOW TO READ THE ISLAND WEATHER

People who venture into Hawai'i's wild, remote places know that weather determines just about everything they do. There are all kinds of natural clocks, compasses and weather indicators to watch and read. Here are a few tips, passed down in the Islands from generation to generation, for forecasting changing weather.

birds fly low

fish swim to surface

◈ If you see lots of cows lying down in an open field, they are getting ready for rain.

◈ If you're pole fishing and the fish are suddenly biting more, rain may be about to arrive. Many fish swim on the surface of the water when there's rain coming. (On very hot days, fish will swim in deeper water where it's cooler—and where they don't bite as often.)

- ◈ Birds fly low before a downpour or squall of rain. They will hunt for insects and bugs just before inclement weather because the insects also stay closer to the ground before bad weather.

- ◈ Birds will sit together and stay close before a storm. Bees will also stay close to their hives.

- ◈ Lots of flies can appear just before a storm.

- ◈ If spiders spin small webs, there might be a storm coming.

- ◈ Many creatures like to move towards water before rainfall.

- ◈ Certain flowers and grasses close up before a rain.

- ◈ Sound seems to magnify before rainfall.

- ◈ A ring around the sun or moon indicates a rain system is approaching.

- ◈ A morning rainbow means morning rain.

- ◈ If rocks are moist or sweating, rain may be coming.

- ◈ If there is dew or moisture on an open field of grass, usually there will be no rain.

- ◈ When stars twinkle a lot, that means the winds are strong up high and there will soon be strong surface winds.

◈ When you can see a million stars at night clearly, the morning will bring dew and moisture, even frost.

◈ Remember the old saying: "Red sky at night, sailor's delight. Red sky in the morning, sailors take warning." It's true in Hawai'i too.

◈ Another old saying: "Campfire smoke close to the ground, storm approaching. Long and rising, good weather approaching or stabilizing."

HOW TO BUILD OR FIND AN OVERNIGHT SHELTER

If you're caught outdoors without a tent, you can build what's called a debris hut or look for an existing sheltered location. One of the great skills you can learn in the bush is the ability to recognize resources and know what you can use in an environment to build or create. This is a very primal skill that stimulates the creative mind through trial-and-error drills. This helps us learn the Hawaiian principles of ‘ike, ‘auana (to explore) and ho‘o (to make happen).

Finding an existing shelter:

◈ Your best bet is to look for a cave. Of course, make sure the cave is safe and unoccupied. Many creatures live in caves. Make a thorough inspection and clean house before moving in.

◈ Deadfall and tree boughs, fallen tree trunks or thick bush and foliage make good cover for overnight.

◈ Rock overhangs, natural terraces and boulders can create crevices big and wide enough to fit between. Make sure there are no loose rocks to fall on you, and that you aren't in or near a riverbed where flash floods can occur!

◈ You can bend a small tree with lots of bushy leaves to make a tree tie-down for shelter.

◈ A natural hollow or depression in the ground can be cleared and covered with grass and leaves and then bordered by rocks.

Making your own:

- ◈ A debris hut uses a stick frame concept to build on. Choose a piece of wood as long as your body plus an extra twelve inches (to allow for movement) as the spine of your hut. Support one end on a convenient tree (see diagram) or pair of sticks crossed at the top and staked down or pounded into the ground. Line up elbow-length (hand to elbow) sticks one to two inches in diameter, working your way up to arm- and leg-length, three to four inches in diameter, along the spine. Make sure their length is sufficient to crisscross over the spine of your hut and allow at least six to eight inches of space between the sticks and your body in the sleeping position to permit turning from one side to the other. Then cover the sticks heavily with twigs and leaves for protection from rain and sun. If it gets cold at night, the compactness of this shelter helps contain your body heat.

- ◈ A beach bed or desert shelter can easily be made by digging a hole or depression deep enough and big enough to fit your body. Line up a poncho or tarp with the depression and use rocks and sand to secure it like a roof. Keep a space for an entrance. If you're at the beach, position this kind of shelter well above the high-water mark!

HOW TO BUILD A SHELTER WITH A PONCHO OR TARP

You can create a temporary shelter with a tarpaulin or a poncho, which are versatile and essential items in any collection of outdoor gear. I never travel into nature without them and highly recommend one or both for your own wilderness survival kit.

Remember:

◈ Never set up shelter over a depression or in any low-lying area vulnerable to flooding when it rains.

◈ Dig a rain trench around your shelter, similar to a moat, for protection from flooding.

◈ Set up any shelter facing the prevailing wind; tent doors should always face the wind.

PONCHO SHELTER

◈ Use two ponchos for this purpose, so that you can connect them with their grommets and snaps to make a larger shelter.

◈ For a one-person shelter: Make a lean-to using two tall forked sticks standing apart like trees in the ground. Find four small sticks for stakes. Hammer two of the stakes through the grommets (use a rock if you don't have a hammer) into the ground on one side of the poncho. Using two pieces of rope, stake down the ropes with the other two stakes to lean your poncho over the two tall sticks and create the lean-to. One side will be open.

◈ For a two-person shelter: Join the two ponchos with their grommets and snaps. You will need eight stakes and enough rope to brace and tie down your connected ponchos to make the tent. Find a stick sturdy enough and long enough to fit the two ponchos. Make a roof joint connecting or tying the long stick to the two forked sticks standing apart like pillars. Close your poncho hood by tying it up (and use it as a pocket too).

TARP SHELTER

◈ A versatile piece for a shelter and many other purposes, a tarp can serve as a makeshift ground cover or a fly or vestibule if you do have a tent.

◈ For a lean-to: Use two adjacent trees as your pillars or stakes, tying your tarp to the trunks of each tree.

◈ For a teepee-style shelter: Create a center pull for the tarp by finding a tree with a sturdy overhead branch. Tie the center of the tarp with a rope to make the pointed top of the teepee. Hoist the rope over and around the limb to lift the tarp to make the teepee. Then stake down the tarp grommets to form a cone-shaped tent.

◈ For a stick frame hut: Using the same design as a debris hut (see page 107), take one long and sturdy trunk-type stick, leaning on two sticks that are crossed and staked down, to make an entrance big enough to slip into. The back end of the long stick will be lying on the ground. Drape the tarp over and stake down both sides through the grommets.

HOW TO MAKE A FIRE PIT

There is an order and a process to making a good fire, including gathering the wood and building a fire pit. In the wild, you will need a handsaw and a keen eye.

Standing dead wood is best because it is dry and ready to burn, compared to fallen dead wood, which can be moist or wet. Living or green wood will not work because it will smoke (which can be useful, sometimes).

◈ Gather the following lengths of kindling when preparing to build your fire pit: Finger-length, "shaka-length" (hand-width), hand-to-elbow, hand-to-shoulder and small-to-medium logs, depending on the size of your fire.

◈ Pile your collected wood sorted by size to make building the fire easier.

Your fire pit must be in an open area, away from bushes and other flammable objects. Be sure to clear the area of any debris, then dig a hole large enough to accommodate your fire.

◈ Leave a clear space around the hole to prevent the fire from jumping and spreading. Some people like to line the rim of the pit with rocks and then clear a two- to three-foot space around this ring of rocks. This creates a good place to sit where the heat from the fire isn't too harsh.

◈ If they're available, place log segments around the pit for seating.

◈ Arrange the firewood you've collected inside the fire pit.

How this is done is important because it determines how long the fire will last, how hot it will burn and how big it will be. Here are two ways to do this:

◇ **Teepee Method:** Starting with the smaller kindling, make a teepee with a door (to insert the tinder bundle) and then progressively add bigger pieces of wood to create a good size teepee. As it burns, the center will fall in, and you can then add more wood as needed.

◇ **Log Cabin Method:** Arrange the kindling in a cabin-style shape around the area where the tinder bundle will be. Think of your Lincoln Log-building days. This method works well in low-wind situations as its shape allows for plenty of airflow.

◇ Be sure to always tend your fire and to have adequate water on hand to extinguish it completely when you're done.

HOW TO MAKE FIRE

I t takes many years and a lot of "dirt time" to become an accomplished traditional firemaker, and there is a certain pride and reverence for the Creator, Mother Nature and our teachers who bestowed us with this beautiful gift. I will share with you the basic rudiments and supplies of attempting to make a fire but remember, realistically, it is silly to think you can learn to make a fire from a book. You need a teacher.

The hand-drilling technique for making fire needs the least amount of equipment. In a survival situation, this basic knowledge will prove valuable. It could be the most incredible contribution you offer your group or for your own personal confidence.

1. In the Hawaiian forest, the wood that will create fire is hau. Learn to recognize what it looks like (see page 70). When you harvest it, be careful to avoid hurting the tree so the next person in need of fire will have what he or she needs.

2. You will need two pieces of wood to rub together and cause friction. Friction will create a coal to start a fire. Both pieces of wood must be of a type that is "friction friendly." (So in Hawai'i, both should be hau.) One piece will become your board, which lays on the ground, and the other piece will be your drill.

3. Cut two straight pieces approximately two feet in length so you have extra. One piece will be wrist- or three-finger width. This will be your board. The other piece should be two-finger width. This will be your drill.

4. Strip the bark from the wood and dry the wood. (You can save the bark dry or soaked to use as binding to tie things.) Here's a secret for determining if it's dry or damp: Press the wood to your lip. If it feels cool, it's still damp.

5. When the wood is dry, split the wood for the board in half. You will now have two pieces of wood for two boards. Shave one or both of the wider sides so that the piece will lay steady on the ground. (It doesn't have to be completely flat, but it can't rock or wobble when you begin pressing on it with the hand drill.)

6. Take the drill piece and shave it down to resemble a pencil point.

7. Next, take your knife and poke the board, twisting just a little to make a tiny hole. (I like to mark the spot by laying my drill flat on top of the board, aligning my knife with the center of the drill. That way you know you will have room for the entire drill point to fit on the board.) This will be where you will place the point of your drill and spin it to—what we call in bush language—"burn a hole." Do this by placing the board on the ground and bracing it with your foot. Take the drill point and place it in the board hole, hold the drill between the center of your palms and, starting from the top of your drill, roll your palms back and forth in a brisk, rapid and rhythmic movement. This will cause the drill to spin into the board and create a friction that will eventually burn a hole into it. This is tricky and takes coordination and correct posture to hold it together.

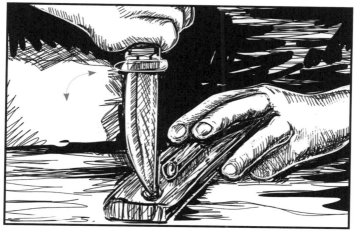

Step 7

Step 8

8. Once you have a decent burn into the shape of your hole, take a break and rest. Now, grab your knife and make a notch at the edge of the board where you made your hole, making a pie-shaped wedge that pierces the circumference of the hole. This is tricky, too; you don't want to enter the hole too much to make a gap that's too big. You also don't want to make it too small where the gap doesn't penetrate the hole. It should end up looking a little like an old-fashioned keyhole. The reason for the gap in the hole is to create an open channel for oxygen to creep in during the friction. Scientifically, oxygen is what ignites the combustion of the friction that creates the heat and eventually the coal.

9. Your last prep is to make a bundle of tinder. In Hawai'i, very dry coconut fibers work best. Strip them and rub them between your palms to break them up. Take your bundle and form it into the shape of a bird's nest. To make it easier to pick up the burning tinder bundle, place it on a piece of 'a'a niu (coconut tree fabric; see page 68) on the ground (make sure it's dry) directly under the hole of your board.

10. Using the same foot placement and technique that you used to burn the hole, spin the drill continuously and rapidly. An individual can do this alone, but working together in a team to take turns drilling (four is a good number) is better—the fire becomes a collective product, plus it's less tiring for any one person. This is hard work!

Step 9

11. The object of this skill is to spin the drill into the board to
create friction between the board and drill until it produces
sufficient heat to be ignited by the oxygen. The fragments
of the wood created by your drilling action will ball up
into a coal. This coal is like an embryo of life and it will
be what will ignite and give birth to fire. When drilling, it
is OK if you pause for a second to reposition your hands at
the top of the drill or for the next person to take their turn

drilling, but if the drill comes out of the hole, you're *pau* (finished). All the built-up energy will escape and you will not be successful in creating a coal. Reposition the drill and start again.

12. When you create a coal, use the point of your knife to roll that coal into the middle of your tinder bundle. Using the 'a'a niu as a carrier, lift it up to your face, breathe very gently and blow some air into the bundle to ignite the coal and tinder bundle into a fire. If it is windy, you can simply lift the bundle into the air and allow the wind to provide the ignition. You will now take that tinder bundle and place it into your firewood in your fire pit and thank the Creator.

THE ART OF MAKING FIRE

Making fire is one of the highest levels of my Hawaiian Inside Tracking survival-training program. My staff of practiced outdoorsmen and women were hesitant to reveal the secrets of fire in these pages. We want everyone to understand that fire is sacred and creating it is an art. (See page 149 for more on this topic.) If you are compelled and inspired to train in the Art of the Sacred Fire, the way we were taught by our elders, we offer that through our HIT program. To learn the Hawaiian story of how fire came to be, you must read the legend of Māui the Demigod and the Secret of Fire.

When you learn the art of making fire, you become the next link in the genealogy of teachers and students. Each teacher in the lineage adds his or her own touches. The use of 'a'a niu as a tinder carrier is unique to the HIT program, an idea developed by Jenny Yagodich. My own teacher, John Stokes, taught me the skill of making fire with the hand drill and bow drill. John, in turn, learned from several different teachers, in particular: Jimmy James, an Australian aboriginal, taught him the hand drill technique; Jose Toledo, a Native American fire maker from New Mexico, taught John to make fire as a team, with four people. This is an important concept that emphasizes teamwork and the idea that fire belongs to us as a community and brings us together to create life; it is not a selfish show-off act.

HOW TO AVOID DEHYDRATION

Take it from me—dehydration can be one of the worst things to endure on a wilderness outing in tropical Hawai'i. Here are some valuable tips to avoid ever getting into that predicament:

KNOWLEDGE

❖ Water, of course, is the key to avoiding dehydration and surviving extreme conditions. You basically can only survive without water for three days. As the Hawaiians say, *ka wai ola* (water is life).

❖ Your body is made up of eighty percent water, which must be replaced constantly due to evaporation, sweat and other bodily functions that shed water.

❖ Water maintains the body's correct temperature, helps you digest food properly and helps your muscles work properly to avoid stiffness.

PREVENTION

❖ Drink lots of water before you begin your journey. If you are properly hydrated, your urine will be clear. Periodic intake of small quantities of water is key when out in the bush. Even if you're not thirsty, small sips are a good idea to maintain fluid balance.

❖ Plan to travel during cool mornings, evenings and nights.

❖ If it's not possible to travel when it's cooler, be sure to drink two to three quarts of water daily.

SYMPTOMS

⬥ Dehydration is body fluid depletion. Watch for thirst, weakness, fatigue, dizziness, headache, fever, dry mouth and nasal passages, and dark-colored urine.

⬥ Look for these behaviors to identify someone experiencing dehydration: Loss of appetite, mental confusion, slurred or stuttered speech, over-emotional stress, slow movements and excessive drowsiness.

HOW TO FIND WATER

Our kūpuna say that we came from the water and we'll go back to the water. The idea of *mālama i ka wai* (to take care of the water) is ingrained in us from small-kid time. Having the knowledge of where to find it is essential in the wild. Some words of water wisdom:

◈ **Discipline:** Once in the wilderness, one of the most important disciplines is not to overdrink. Avoid big gulps and take little sips to ration water. In a survival situation, just a taste can help you get by.

◈ **Packing:** When planning a hike or camping trip into an area without running water, you'll need to pack as much drinking water as you can comfortably carry.

◈ **Storing:** If you plan to return to the same area, here's an *akamai* (smart) idea taught to me by a wise Hawaiian who traveled to the island of Kahoʻolawe, which has no natural supply of fresh water. On a return trip, he buried water safely in different spots in gulches and valleys to ensure that he had a supply for the next trip.

The best way to secure water in the wild is to collect rainwater, which is already fresh and clean. But rain, of course, is undependable, especially during Hawaiʻi's long dry season. Here are other ways to find water:

IN THE FOREST

◈ Follow the animal trails, especially the ones that lead down into gulches (which are formed by water) and eventually to a water source.

- ◈ Look for insects like bees and flies. The water that they also need is usually within flying range. Watch where they go and try to follow.

- ◈ Find rivers and streams.

- ◈ In the rainforest, look for water dripping at the base of a *pali* (cliff).

- ◈ Locate the water table beneath especially verdant areas. You need dig only a foot or two before the water will start to pool in the hole.

- ◈ Look for plants that serve as water carriers for standing water. Plants like bamboo and cactus hold water in their trunks or stems. Certain bromeliads have cup-like structures that allow water to pool.

- ◈ Lick the dew from leaves.

- ◈ Squeeze water out of rotting wood, which often serves as a sponge.

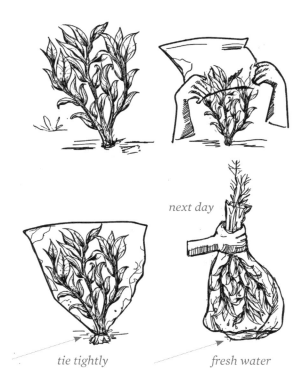

next day

tie tightly   *fresh water*

◈ Collect water in the form of condensation from plants. Cover a plant with a plastic bag, securing it tightly around the plant's base. The heat and moisture of the plant will cause condensation to form on the inside of the bag. When you're ready to collect the water, bend the plant over so the water collects in the bottom of the bag to avoid spilling it when you remove the bag. Or find a plant that's already bent over, so that the water will readily collect in the bottom of the bag.

ocean

100 feet inland → *dig here.*

rocks act as filter

fresh water

NEAR THE OCEAN

◈ Find the vegetation line and dig for a water table, which is usually over the first hill or dune where the land levels off and plants start to grow—about one hundred feet from the shore. Look for a sand depression and start digging. This water is usually fresh because the rocks act as a filter for the seawater.

◈ Look for rainwater (not seawater) left in holes in rocks.

◈ Use a container to collect fresh water flowing from springs beneath the ocean's surface, usually about ten feet down. You'll know when you've found one because the clear ocean water will look cloudy. Dive down with the cap on your container, turn the container over the spring, uncap and let the fresh water suck into the container.

WATER CONTAMINATION

It is very important to make sure that your drinking water is not contaminated. You can get very sick if it is. Some clear signs that water is contaminated:

⬦ It is stagnant.

⬦ It has foam or bubbles.

⬦ It has an odor.

⬦ It is discolored, muddy or cloudy.

⬦ It has dead organisms in it.

Cleansing: Even if it doesn't look contaminated, you still need to clean or purify the water you collect. There are many different ways to do this, some traditional and some more modern.

⬦ Boil the water for at least ten minutes.

⬦ Use purification tablets, which can be bought at an outdoor or sporting goods store.

⬦ Add iodine, eight drops per quart of water, stir and let sit for ten minutes.

⬦ Use a water filter cup, which filters with charcoal.

⬦ There are now many high-tech, ready-to-go water filter bottles and other accessories available at outdoor-supply stores.

"OUR KŪPUNA SAY THAT WE CAME
FROM THE WATER AND WE'LL GO BACK
TO THE WATER."

HOW TO PREVENT, DETECT AND TREAT HYPOTHERMIA

Even in the tropics, hypothermia can be a serious survival issue. In simple terms, the condition refers to a dangerous loss of normal (98°F) body temperature. When the body gets too cold, the flow of blood slows down in fingers and toes and moves to conserve the heat needed for vital organs. This causes a drop in body temperature and creates a potentially dangerous imbalance. Here are some tips for identifying, preventing and treating hypothermia:

CAUSES

◇ Wet and cold, windy conditions

◇ Lack of food and sleep (these can lead to poor mental state and low energy, which make things worse)

◇ Improper attire

◇ Inexperience with inclement outdoor weather conditions

SYMPTOMS

◇ Shivering at 95°F

◇ Shaky hands

◇ Incoherent or nonsensical speech

◇ Confusion

◇ Exhaustion and drowsiness

◇ Lack of physical coordination: clumsy and stumbling

- ◈ Tense and rigid muscles
- ◈ Slow pulse and heartbeat, difficulty breathing, shallow respiration
- ◈ Unconsciousness, coma and finally, death

PREVENTION

- ◈ Stay dry, avoid wind and cold; eat and rest well; keep the mind and body active.
- ◈ Always have extra dry clothing.
- ◈ Stop the outing and turn back to seek medical help at the first sign of symptoms. Do not continue on.
- ◈ Seek shelter immediately if there is the possibility of hypothermia.

TREATMENT

- ◈ Remove afflicted person from inclement weather to shelter and warmth immediately.
- ◈ Remove and replace wet clothing with dry, and/or wrap victim with sleeping bag and blankets.
- ◈ If victim is conscious, raise the internal body core temperature with a warm drink or with steam inhaled from boiled water.
- ◈ In an extreme situation, use your own body warmth by wrapping your body around victim like a blanket.

HOW TO GUARD AGAINST LEPTOSPIROSIS

While traveling outdoors in Hawai'i, especially in rainforests and off the beaten path, you will likely cross rivers and streams and encounter waterfalls, ponds, mudflats and swampy areas. Be aware of exposure to the leptospirosis, an infectious disease caused by the spirochete bacteria, which is widespread throughout the Hawaiian islands.

Spirochete bacteria

- Animals carry the bacteria, which can be transmitted to humans through contact with soil and water contaminated by the waste of animal carriers, such as rats, mice, mongoose and wild pigs.

- Humans can contract the bacteria through open cuts, broken skin and mucous membranes in the eyes, nose and mouth.

- If a forest area or stream looks polluted or might be contaminated with animal waste matter, do not enter the area, and do not wash or drink from the stream. If you have an open cut or exposed area of skin, absolutely do not step into the water or mud, take a swim or even dip your head underwater. Such exposure could put you in potential danger of contracting this dangerous bacteria.

- If you are exposed, symptoms will appear within two to twenty-five days of contact with the infected animal waste. These flu-like symptoms include headaches, muscle aches, fever, chills and eye pain when exposed to bright light. Seek medical attention right away, as high doses of penicillin and antibiotics will need to be administered for recovery.

- Untreated leptospirosis infection can lead to kidney disease, jaundice, meningitis and even death.

HOW TO BRUSH YOUR TEETH IN THE WILDERNESS

There are some very cool ways to take care of your teeth in the wilderness. While there are several reasons to do this the bush way, one of them is avoiding the odor of toothpaste on your breath or body when you are tracking, hunting or harvesting in the wild. It's a dead giveaway to most animals, which can smell, see and sense things much better than you can. And while you're at it, use unscented dental floss too. Here are three simple ways to take care of this personal grooming task:

◈ Carry some baking soda as part of your survival pack and use a little to swirl around in your mouth, brush your teeth and then rinse with some water.

◈ Take some charcoal embers from your campfire. Mix with a little water, swirl in your mouth and brush. Then spit out and rinse. Do not swallow.

◈ Perhaps the easiest way to keep your teeth clean was taught to me by master bushman John Stokes, who learned it from aboriginals. Rub and scrub your teeth with your tongue continuously, getting into all areas of your mouth until you develop a mouthful of saliva. (Did you know that saliva is medicinal?) Then slowly swallow, little by little, until it's all gone. This also acts as a medicinal elixir for your throat and the linings of your organs.

HOW TO TREAT DIARRHEA, HAWAIIAN-STYLE

Diarrhea happens—especially out in the bush under unfamiliar living conditions and with changes in eating and drinking habits. To help your body adjust, be sure to drink lots of water to stay hydrated.

◈ Diarrhea usually results from drinking untreated water or eating undercooked or raw food, including vegetables, meat and shellfish. You want to avoid any serious digestive illness in the wilderness, such as that transmitted by *E. coli* bacteria.

◈ To be safe, purify your water and thoroughly cook all food, then wash your dishes and utensils with the purified water.

◈ For diarrhea, try the following remedies:

  ◇ Use ashes from your campfire to make a tea to drink.

  ◇ Use laukahi leaves to brew another tea that's a strong astringent.

  ◇ Look for young guava shoots close to the ground and eat a few.

HOW TO TREAT AN UPSET STOMACH

Entering the wilderness can de-stress, detox and cleanse you. An Amazon medicine man once told my tracker friend John Stokes that as soon as you enter the rainforest you are already healing. But sometimes you can get an upset stomach from the change to different foods and environments in the outdoors. Here are some tips to avoid and treat an upset stomach while traveling in the wilderness:

PREVENTION

◈ Before going into the wild, hydrate with lots of water.

◈ Start eating sensibly a day or two before: Consume good carbohydrates for fuel and just enough protein and veggies for energy and strength.

◈ Avoid rich and processed foods.

REMEDIES

◈ Pack some baking soda and mix with water to drink.

◈ Find young guava shoots to pick and eat.

◈ Brew a tea from charcoal embers from a campfire mixed with water to create a soothing elixir.

◈ Suck on a lemon wedge for nausea or upset stomach.

◈ Carry an apple in your pack. It works for an upset stomach as well as a nutritious snack.

◈ Find a wild banana patch. Bananas are another natural remedy for an upset stomach and are among the tropical fruits found in wild in Hawai'i's rain forests.

◈ Look for ginger root, a well-known and natural remedy for nausea, motion sickness and upset stomachs. The root can be chewed or brewed into a tea. An option is to carry ginger candy or seed available in Chinatown shops. Just watch the added sugar.

◈ Carry and munch on plain soda crackers.

◈ Dab a little peppermint oil under your nostrils for nausea.

HOW TO TREAT AN INSECT BITE

As you'd expect, Hawai'i has its share of tropical insects and other pests. Here are some common critters and remedies in the event of a bite or sting:

MOSQUITOES

◈ Avoid damp conditions, stagnant water and swampy areas where mosquitoes can multiply.

◈ If bitten, try not to scratch to avoid swelling and breaking the skin, which increases the possibility of infection.

◈ Rub an over-the-counter antihistamine cream or calamine lotion on the area to reduce the itch.

◈ For a natural remedy, laukahi leaves can be pounded or chewed to produce a padding to be applied on bites.

◈ You can also chew the tiny pollen particles of the laukahi flower to develop a natural body repellent, full of vitamin B, which stops mosquitoes from biting you.

BEES, YELLOW JACKETS, WASPS AND HORNETS

◈ Honeybees only sting once, leave behind their barbed stinger and then die. If you can see the stinger, try to remove it immediately by carefully scraping it out with your fingernail. If it isn't removed, the stinger will continue to inject venom for another couple minutes.

◈ Wasps, yellow jackets and hornets, on the other hand,

Laukahi flower

do not leave behind their smooth stingers and can sting multiple times. Crushing one of these nasty insects will release the venom smell, and others will likely follow, launching an angry attack.

◈ Common remedies include a mud pack, ice and cold compress, meat tenderizer, calamine lotion, baking soda pack, laukahi pack (see above) and even an aspirin rubbed on a sting area that's been dampened.

◈ If you are stung in the throat or mouth, seek emergency medical help immediately. The venom will cause swelling in the throat and mouth that can block your breathing passages.

CENTIPEDES AND SCORPIONS

◈ These insect bites can be much more serious than a mosquito or bee sting. To be safe, seek medical attention immediately.

- ◈ Avoidance is your best bet. Stay away from piles of wood or leaves. Pay attention to what you grab or where you step when cleaning, harvesting or moving anything in the wild.

- ◈ Don't set up your tent close to rock crevices or rock walls, usually the home of centipedes.

- ◈ Make it a good bush habit to shake out clothing, towels, bedding or other materials that have been hanging, lying or piled up on any surface, where it can be a snug home for one of these critters. (I once found a small scorpion in my camouflage jacket, as I was getting ready to go hunting.)

- ◈ Lastly, make sure your tent door is always zippered shut to prevent bugs and creatures from crawling or flying into your living space to bite or sting you.

HOW TO USE THE MOON

*M*ahina, the moon, is our calendar. We look up at the sky and study the moon and its phases. We learn its different faces. We name them by each night and we mathematically put them into an order that connects us to our land and ocean, and teaches us what happens as the moon governs the tides and cycles of the Earth Mother. By the moon, we know the best and worst times to plant our crops and go fishing in the different sections of our surrounding ocean. We were taught from childhood that the moon was our grandmother, our tūtū wahine, and she would guide us to behave correctly and do the *pono* or right things throughout the night.

Back in the day, we were all taught to memorize the Hawaiian moon calendar. There were several mahina chants or nursery rhyme-type melodies that our kūpuna would teach us to learn the cycles and the phases of the moon. The Hawaiian calendar is marked off by lunar months which are grouped into two seasons: *Kau wela* (dry) and *Ho'oilo* (wet). Sun and rain, so simple! Kau wela roughly corresponds to May to November on the Gregorian calendar, while Ho'oilo spans to May. Each lunar month starts with a new moon and ends on a night with no moon. Depending on the season and month, certain plants or fish are more abundant or are kapu to maintain sustainability.

Kau wela (Dry Season) begins with the first new moon in May. During this season, low tides happen during the day. The weather is generally warm, cooled by trade winds. Plants grow rapidly during the long days.

◈ *Ikiiki*—This first month of Kau wela is a warm and

humid month; the name itself means "acute discomfort." A good time to fish for *pāpio* (young jack or trevally), *weke* (goatfish), *moi* (Pacific threadfin), *uhu* (parrotfish) or *akule* (big-eye scad). *Honu* (green sea turtle) nesting begins. Do not disturb turtles at any time; they are a protected species.

◈ *Ka'aona*—Peak spawning begins for moi and uhu; harvesting these fish is now kapu.

◈ *Hinaia'ele'ele*—During this hot month, sudden storms are a possibility. You will often see dark clouds over the mountains.

◈ *Mahoe Mua*—This is a month of changing weather with periods of rain and wind alternating with sun. Likewise, the ocean is rough and then calm. Fishing is good, especially for *a'u* (swordfish), but keep an eye out for storms.

◈ *Mahoe Hope*—Weather will grow rougher, with more rain showers, during this month, but there are still good days to fish (especially deep-ocean) and harvest before the wet season begins.

◈ *'Ikuwā* (or *'Ikuā*)—Both words mean "noisy," which refers to the sound of the wind, rain, thunder and lightning that marks this month. The four-month *Makahiki* period, a time of festivities and a kapu on war, begins.

Ho'oilo (Wet Season) begins with the first new moon in November. During this season, low tides occur at night. The weather is cooler and nights are longer.

◇ *Welehu*—Storms come from the south during this first month of Hoʻoilo and the water appears murky. Not a very good time for fishing or any other outdoor activities.

◇ *Makaliʻi*—This is the final month of honu nesting in Hawaiʻi. It is a wet month with Kona winds (coming from a southwesterly direction, the opposite of our usual trade winds).

◇ *Kāʻelo*—"*Elo*" means saturated, which is appropriate for this wet, stormy month. *Ula* (Hawaiian spiny lobster) come out on the reef at night during the full moon high tide.

◇ *Kaulua*—Although the weather is stormy, good fishing can be found on the reef and close to shore. *Kūmū* (goatfish) and *ulua* (jack or trevally) are among the fish that are plentiful.

◇ *Nana*—Rain is still plentiful, but there are many sunny days now. In addition to the fish found during Kaulua, other reef and shoreline fish grow plentiful. *Āholehole* (young Hawaiiain flagtail), however, are in their peak spawning period and are kapu.

◇ *Welo*—This month marks the end of the wet season. Deep sea and reef fishing are both excellent.

Each month is further divided into three *anahulu* or periods of ten nights. Within those periods, as with the months themselves, each night has its own name and activities that are recommended or cautioned against. Some of those nights are grouped together into periods of three or four nights which have similar characteristics.

The calendar can get very specific, but here are some general key times that are useful to know if you'll be hunting, fishing or camping:

Hoʻonui or "Rising" Anahulu (Nights 1 through 10)

◈ *Hilo* (Night 1)—During a new moon night, fish hide in the reefs and deep-sea fishing is good.

◈ *Kū* (Nights 3 through 6)—The four nights of Kū are a good time for fishing, but if you are setting out on a long sail, be aware that ocean currents will change soon.

◈ *ʻOle* (Nights 7 through 10; Nights 21 through 23)—ʻOle means "nothing," and these periods are considered unproductive. Tides are dangerous and high; the sea is rough, fishing is not good and jellyfish are abundant during the eighth through tenth days on certain shores. It is a very windy time.

Poepoe or "Full" Anahulu (Nights 11 through 20)

◈ *Huna* (Night 11)—Huna means "hidden" and on this night you will find fish hiding in their holes.

◈ *Hua* (Night 13)—This is the first full moon night of the month. The moon will appear egg-shaped (hua means "egg") and it is a bountiful time. *Ipu* (gourds) are abundant on the *ʻaina* (land) and fish are plentiful at sea.

◈ *Hoku* (Night 15)—The moon on this night is thought to be the true full moon, the most full. *Hoku kua* means "lined up close together" and root plants and bananas (which grow in this manner) are plentiful.

◈ *Mahealani* (Night 16)—The last of the full moon nights. Currents are strong but fishing is still good.

◈ *Kulu* (Night 17)—Bananas are easy to find now because the sheath covering the fruit drops off on this night. It is also a good time for potatoes and melons. It is a traditional time for making offerings from the first fruits of the season, so you know edible plants are plentiful.

◈ *Lāʻau* (Nights 18 through 20)—These are the tree nights. A favorable time for planting certain things and also for fishing. It is also a good time for gathering medicinal herbs and plants.

Emi or "Diminishing" Anahulu (Nights 21 through 30)

◈ ʻOle (Nights 21 through 23)—see above

◈ *Kāloa* (Nights 24 through 26)—These are good fishing nights. *Makaloa* (a type of shellfish) and *ʻolē* (conch shell) are plentiful.

◈ *Mauli* (Night 29)—Beginning with *Kane* two nights before, the moon doesn't rise until dawn. By Mauli, it doesn't rise until it is already daylight. Tides are low on this dark night and it is a good time to fish.

◈ *Muku* (Night 30)—Another dark night, good for fishing.

HOW TO FIT IN WITH THE LOCALS

E ven if you were born and raised in Hawai'i, once you step outside your neighborhood or your comfort zone, you're in someone else's territory. You're not a "local" anymore. You've got to learn how to fit in. The survival skills of adjusting, adapting, blending and being aware are just as important when you visit a new neighborhood as when you go out in the forest. On a personal level, this is one of the greatest survival techniques you could ever learn and practice in both the natural world and the urban environment. From the time I was a child, I was always fascinated with survivalist objects, but also about how I could communicate with others. To me, survival is really about co-existing.

◈ Pay attention to your surroundings when you are in a new environment. Watch for places like dark street corners or how a nice part of town changes into a shadier area on the outskirts.

◈ Be aware of your posture and swagger. You must remember, no matter how confident you may be of your abilities, you still appear to be trespassing.

◈ We don't want a confrontation; we want a greeting and permission to enter.

◈ We can do without aggressiveness. This doesn't only mean in a physical sense, but verbal pushiness, too, and even extends to aggressive consumption. Think of it this way: What if you are diving in a good dive spot and you aggressively take a lot of fish, stringing them on your towline, making a big bloody trail in the water? For one thing, everyone will be mad at you for taking all the fish. But you also mark yourself as prey for predators—animal and human—who want what you have.

◈ In Hawai'i and most islands around the world, the feeling and vibe is "laid back." Try to embody that and match that rhythm; otherwise it will be very clear you're not local.

In Hawai'i, survival means more than the physical skills of finding food or shelter or fighting off predators. True survival goes deeper. It is about our relationships with other people as well as with nature. Survival and aloha go hand in hand. On the following pages are reflections from Hawaiian Inside Tracking staff on survival and the various forms it can take.

APPENDICES

ONE THROW

by Palakiko Yagodich

The story of the *'upena kiloi*, or throw net, is known across the world
As many cultures practice this sacred art form.

Here in Hawai'i, 'upena kiloi is also a valued traditional skill.

The ability to feed people in one throw is something to think of.

Passed down from uncles to nephew, this great knowledge lives in
the family.

That knowledge becomes wisdom when that nephew passes it to
his son.

And wisdom of the 'upena kiloi becomes a tradition when that son

Is able to feed others

In one throw.

*Palakiko Yagodich is an instructor and trainer for the Hōe'a
Initiative's Hawaiian Inside Tracking program. Originally from
Maui, he currently resides on the north shore of O'ahu. He is a
graduate of a four-year mentorship training program of The Tracking
Project (Corrales, New Mexico) and Hawaiian Inside Tracking, and
has worked for Hō'ea Initiative since 2008.*

SACRED FIRE

by Jennifer Yagodich

There are several different types of fire. There's the backyard barbecue kind, lit by using a match and as much lighter fluid as possible—the kind that blazes just long enough to cook your burgers and hot dogs, is calmed with douses of beer and then finally put out with the garden hose. There's the all-natural kind, the kind that is started by Mother Nature herself in the form of molten lava or lightning. There's the electrical kind, the chemical kind and even the kind that starts when sunlight reflects off of certain surfaces. The worst kind is the on-purpose kind, used for intentional destruction.

But the kind I refer to here is the sacred kind. This is the most special kind of fire—the kind our primitive ancestors relied on for life, the kind you create using your own energy—the fire you respect and feed. This kind of fire is a gift. This kind of fire is beautiful. Most importantly, though, this kind of fire is hard to make. There's an entire process to making sacred fire; the whole thing, from start to finish, is a ceremony.

The first time I actually made a sacred fire with a bow and drill, it took me about an hour and a half—after already trying over a period of months without success. I made a lot of smoke during that time and even a few coals, but I never birthed fire. It was so frustrating. I wanted to give up but am so glad I didn't, because one day it happened. I was given the gift of fire: I breathed life into it and there it was—a beautiful flame that I created with my own two hands, one that could provide me with warmth, protect me from predators, cook my food and boil my water. But most of all, it was a fire that empowered me forever. I know that sounds kooky, but it's the truth. There's something very satisfying about knowing that I can make fire.

Guidebooks, scout lessons, military training and survival shows can tell you how to make fire. Get a couple pieces of wood, they say, rub them together and you will make fire. They may be right, but they're leaving out the most important parts, like how to correctly harvest the wood, how to *pule* (pray) for that life, how to find the wood that has mana (energy).

Remember, to native Hawaiians this is sacred fire. There is so much that goes into it. Sure, you can use other ways to make fire, and in a survival situation you'll do whatever it takes to make one. However, our mindset is to be able to create a sacred fire using natural materials the way our ancestors did. In Hawai'i, the secret of fire was taken from the *'alae 'ula* (Hawaiian mudhen) by Māui the demigod. Coincidentally, this is the same method favored by Native Americans—using soft woods to form a coal. It's important to be able to correctly identify the resources needed to create a fire, especially in a survival situation.

Personally, I am always prepared with a fire kit whenever I go out into the wild—I never have to search and hope for the right materials. This is one of our teachings, and I'm honored to be able to teach others the art of making sacred fire. Join our program sometime and I'll be happy to share it with you, too!

Jenny Yagodich is an instructor and trainer for the Hōeʻa Initiative's Hawaiian Inside Tracking program. Born in Monterey, California, the daughter of a military family, Jenny has lived in Hawaiʻi from the age of twelve. Jenny first met Brother Noland as a participant in the Pacific American Foundation's NAPALI Leadership program. She is also a graduate of The Tracking Project (Corrales, New Mexico) and of Hawaiian Inside Tracking's four-year mentorship program.

SUSTAINABLE ALOHA
by Pomai Weigert

I n life, when we are in the wild places of the world—even our
own heads!—there are some things we're never prepared for:
death, natural disaster, terminal illness, depression, failure, losing
a job, losing a loved one and just losing our way, among others. And
though all of our physical training has been excellent, and we might
feel we have completed and learned all that we can, it is at this very
moment that the universe can bring us face to face with our true
selves—our true abilities and true fears, life's greatest challenges,
heartbreaks and expectations. It is here, at our most vulnerable,
where we learn Sustainable Aloha.

"Sustainable" by definition means our ability to maintain or keep
going.

"Aloha" in the Hawaiian culture has many interpretations but in
this case means "breath of life" and "unconditional love."

Essentially, Sustainable Aloha is our connection to everything
else, physical and otherwise, and our survival as a human culture
relies on it deeply. It is the foundation we are built upon as strong
and enlightened spirits. It is the strength beyond the body. It is
our humanity, our character and our integrity. It is the power to
overcome logic, limitation and doubt even in the darkest of times
and the longest of hours. It is our strongest resort and our highest
level of hope. It is the ancient and unbreakable understanding
that there is light at the end of every tunnel and gratitude in every
struggle. It is our power to forgive and to move forward. It is our
ability to love with our whole heart and "bring things together"

even when the odds are against us—especially when the odds are against us. It is the courage and commitment to keep going, to keep fighting, to rise up and keep believing in the good and in each other. And when we feel like there is nothing left to give, Sustainable Aloha will be there to save us—to keep us alive. It lives within us, protecting and guiding us always.

Sustainable Aloha is the spiritual aspect to our survival. It is the part of our existence that cannot be physically seen but is revealed in our actions and interactions with ourselves, our community and our environment. It is the strength a mother has when protecting her children. It is the fortitude a family has when a home is broken. It is the bond a community has during chaos. It is the resilience a nation has in wartime. It is what keeps us going when we are hungry, angry, lonely or tired. It is the intuitive and inherent knowledge that if we love something, we will never give up on it, and we will share this love for generation upon generation.

Pomai Weigert hails from a multi-generational, family-owned, native Hawaiian agritourism business in Hawai'i. Besides working for this family company, she is a workshop trainer for the Hawai'i Agritourism Association. As Brother Noland's daughter, she has absorbed his teachings throughout her life and is also a graduate of The Tracking Project (Corrales, New Mexico) and of Hawaiian Inside Tracking's mentorship program.

SURVIVAL IS KNOWING PEOPLE

by Brother Noland

Survival is about more than just physical skills. People who travel, for example, often develop relationships with others that can turn into lifelong friendships. Sometimes we cross paths with people with whom we connect for a specific capsule of time and create unforgettable moments, even if we never see them again. To me, a big-time survival technique is what I call the Art of Living.

This important survival tool means learning to live correctly and behave well—so that you don't find yourself in predicaments that put you in grave survival situations. When you practice the Art of Living, you soon find that you can count on others. People enjoy working with you and for you; your fellowship is always good company. You can go to a new place and the local people will guide you and share with you their cultural ways, because you can engage with others and appreciate their lifestyle.

I think you can see how this can be an excellent survival technique. According to Harvard University professor Dr. Howard Gardner, author of the great book *Frames of Mind: The Theory of Multiple Intelligences*, what I call the Art of Living is your inter-personal and intra-personal intelligences at work. It is knowing how to communicate and get along with others, and knowing how to communicate with your inner self so that you can talk to and teach yourself. With these two skills, you cultivate self-confidence, and the decisions you make will be on point. In a survival situation, what enables you to survive is your attitude and state of mind—your willpower and your refusal to give up. Under challenging circumstances, it is important to project this kind of energy around others, especially if they are weakened and cannot assert themselves as they would like to. Developing these skills improves your chances of making good choices, which ultimately allows you to enjoy life—rather than simply endure its calamities and misfortunes.

ACKNOWLEDGMENTS

Nānā i ke Kumu
Observe the Teacher, Look to the Source

During my journey, many teachers have helped me bring my work full circle. As I continue to learn, liberate and manifest myself, I am honored to represent and share their great knowledge, wisdom and aloha. Each one of my programs, my camps and my students document and reflect the combined influence of all my teachers and their teachers—a kaleidoscope of cultural wisdom. I am grateful.

Dad—you opened the path for me. Kali Master Frank Mamalias, Walter Ritte Jr., Kaipo Daniels, Moku Buchanan, John Stokes, Kumu Tony Conjugacion, Sid Daguman, Richard Bulacan, Gary Rapozo, Arnold Hiura, James Bacon, Duane Kurisu, Nana Veary, Ellen Kusano, Lloyd Stern, Mac Poepoe, Mike Ka'awa, Donnie Martin Jr., Amy Hiura, Juanito Dudoit, Miller Maioho, Kata Maduli, Rex Niimoto, Katherine Ka'ahanui Medina, Jeff Grundhauser, Nana and Grandpa Raymond Pante, Red and Laurie Walser, Mom and Sis, the Daniels 'ohana of Waimea, the Ako 'ohana, the Kam 'ohana, the Onaka 'ohana, the Ritte 'ohana, the 'ohana of The Tracking Project, my musical 'ohana, the souls and spirits of the people of northern Japan and so many more.

My dedicated and loyal HIT staff—Jennifer Yagodich, Palakiko Yagodich, Pomai Weigert and Mele Coelho. And you, Setsumi—over the past three years of knowledge and wisdom, I have learned so much about me through you. The "beautiful season" is embodied in the survival spirit of the mind and heart.